CLARITY WIN$

Steve Woodruff

Published in the USA

Printed in the USA

First Edition

ISBN: 978-1-7328571-0-0

Layout and design: Swish Design

This book is dedicated to the memory of Esther Woodruff.

Wife of one; mother of four; grandmother, teacher, and friend of many.

She loved well.

Lots of people are applauding *Clarity Wins*...

"What if you could re-wire your prospects' brains to remember your business and what it offers — using words alone? Steve Woodruff more than delivers on this tantalizing promise in *Clarity Wins*. You're about to learn at the feet of the King of Clarity — and you're in for a treat!"
–Pamela Wilson, founder of BIG Brand System

"*Clarity Wins* is a winner! Steve Woodruff brings together amazing stories and anecdotes to help the reader clearly see a better way to succeed. A must read for all business leaders."
–Jim Trunick, Partner at AIIR Consulting and author of *The CORE of Leadership™*

"My agency has specialized in helping clients define and live out their brand for 25+ years, and that discipline is more important today than ever. Steve's book helps organizations define who they are and why it matters. In this crowded and noisy world, clarity is the key to success - it really is that simple."
–Drew McLellan, Principal, Agency Management Institute and co-editor of *Age of Conversation*

"Steve's clarity principles saved me from targeting the wrong companies, and potentially losing prospects who could become very valuable clients. Most importantly, now my messaging is clear and focused, and I'm comfortable delivering it. I am so grateful for his wizardry!"
–Marina Erulkar, Principal, Hampstead Solutions LLC

But, of course, not everyone is a fan.

"Insufficiently verbose. It's 750 pages short of a true classic."
—Leo Tolstoy, Author, War and Peace

"Does not leverage agile frameworks to provide a robust synopsis for optimal enterprise-wide deployment. Needs more scalable iterative approaches to corporate strategy vis a vis fostering collaborative thinking to further the overall value proposition. We prefer a world view of disruptive ambiguity."
—J. Argon, Chief Obfuscation Officer, Spueing, Fogg and Smoak

"This book about getting to the point is for losers. Abe Lincoln came to Gettysburg and spoke for just two minutes. I lit up that stage for two entire hours. Clearly, I won."
—Edward Everett, memorable 19th century orator

"Niche thinking? Pigeonholing oneself? Pffffft! I prefer to cast a wide net and keep all my options open."
—Jack O. Falltrades, barista-in-training and professional couch surfer

CONTENTS

CLARITY
WIN$

Steve Woodruff

FOREWORD

by Josh Bernoff

Life is a muddle.

Life is filled with misunderstandings, loved ones who change their minds, children, pets, flat tires, presidential elections, and any number of other sources of chaos and confusion. The chaos is inescapable.

Business is no different. If anything, it's worse. In most companies, people who work together to generate a profit operate in a barely controlled manner. Those same companies pay consultants millions of dollars to create "identities" for themselves and then, for the most part, operate in a way that undermines those carefully curated identities. Market strategies and messages are muddled. No one really questions this; it seems to just be part of the air we breathe in the business world. It's background noise.

At least no one questioned it until Steve Woodruff came along.

Steve is a really nice guy who is also really smart. (It's amazing how infrequently those two qualities go together.) More to the point: Steve is clear. He is clear about who he is, what he does, and how it helps people. Steve is the King of Clarity.

Steve shares a simple but powerful insight: clarity creates referrals.

If you pick a specific target market, identify how you can help people in that market, and follow through, you will have happy clients. But happy clients, in themselves, are not enough.

You want happy clients *who can refer you*. Clients who will say, “Ah, yes; when it comes to copy editing business books, Merlina is the best there is.” Or “You need to integrate your Web site with Salesforce? You really should talk to the people at Cloud Widget.”

Or “You need help with clarity and referrals? Talk to Steve Woodruff.”

Referrals are more important than search engine optimization. They’re more important than digital advertising, your LinkedIn description (which is probably lame), your tweets, what shoes you wear, or how firm your handshake is. Referrals are the direct path from doing a good job to getting more business. And the reason you’re not getting more of them is that people don’t know how to describe what you do — because you don’t know how to describe what you do. This book helps with that.

This is an easy book to consume. It’s simple and short and logical. It would be easy to read it, smile, and then go on with your chaotic day and do everything the same way you have been.

Please don’t do that.

Here’s what you should do.

First, read these pages and take notes about what this means to you, your career, and your business. Go ahead, highlight and dog-ear the pages (or whatever passes for those actions in the eBook version).

Pigeonhole yourself (yes, you read that right — *Clarity Wins* teaches you how to do that — and why you should).

Stop doing lots of things sorta okay and start doing a few things — or one thing — really well.

Craft a memorable message that's easy to pass along.

Then you'll start to see clients multiply.

Life is a muddle. But your work doesn't have to be. Clarity not only generates business, it feels great.

So stop fooling around and get to work on it.

— Josh Bernoff, author, Writing Without Bullshit

PART 1

The Greatest Business Challenge

INTRODUCTION

Knowing your Enemy

If you're in business, you're in a battle. You're advancing, retreating, strategizing, reacting, digging in, re-deploying — it can be exhausting in those trenches. As you look at your fluctuating bank balance, you're constantly reminded that the stakes are much higher than the playground disputes of your youth.

And when you feel like your side might be losing — well, join the club. Many of your fellow business leaders regularly feel the same way. Oftentimes, the setbacks seem to outnumber the breakthroughs.

Business-building is not for the faint of heart.

In an ideal world, a logical formula would get us straight to success. Something like this:

- You have something people need or want.
- You find the customers with those needs and communicate your offer clearly to them.
- You make a transaction that's a win-win, exchanging money for value.
- Lather, rinse, repeat.

- Retire to beachside resort.

Easy, right? Except we live in the real world, not fantasyland. Unrealistic success formulas rarely make the cash register ring, except for the endless stream of business snake oil salesmen hawking them.

According to the Small Business Administration, only half of all new establishments are still operating after 5 years and only 30% after 10 years. Businesses struggle to succeed simply because providers and buyers often fail to connect.

Why is that? Because we're not getting heard. We're not breaking through. We struggle to find the customers that need us, and they don't even know we exist. That smooth highway to success we dreamed about is actually an uneven track filled with hurdles and opposition. It's muddled out there.

The path between developing your product or service and earning revenue from a convinced customer is full of complications. Yes, there are exceptional companies that immediately attract customers and accelerate rapidly from the outset. But that's probably not us. While they get the headlines, you and I are more likely to be in the 99.9% of small businesses that do hand-to-hand battle to survive and grow every day.

Surprisingly, however, identifying the *main opposition* that 99.9% of all businesses face is actually a very easy task. We can, in the immortal advice of Sun Tzu's Art of War, know our enemy. Who is that enemy? To understand what you're up against, let's look back at a familiar story, featuring an unfair battle with a truly nasty opponent.

CHAPTER 1

Facing the Enemy

In the famous biblical story of David and Goliath, a shepherd boy armed only with a sling and a stone takes on a fearsome, armored giant. This massive opponent has been threatening and cursing David's countrymen for days, and Israel's army is shrinking from the battle. The game appeared to be over before it was set to begin.

Taking on such an opponent was inconceivable.

Then David shows up. Unlike his older brothers, he is still too young for the army. He owns no sword, no shield. Nonetheless, he takes one look at Goliath, listens to his loud bluster, and decides to take him on. Silly David — definitely not paying attention to the tribal oddsmakers.

David even refuses to wear his king's armor or to pick up any of the more advanced weaponry offered to him. Those weren't a "fit" for how he does battle. Instead, he goes out with a sling, some stones, and…his secret weapon.

No laser. No nuke. Instead, that upstart shepherd boy has one awesome skill. He could pinpoint, and hit, bullseyes.

David, though terribly outgunned, is really, really good at precision targeting. Everyone else sees an impregnable enemy, with shields up and weapons charged. David, however, sees a bullseye painted on Goliath's exposed forehead, just waiting to be penetrated by a simple stone from his sling.

> *"What the Israelites saw, from high on the ridge, was an intimidating giant. In reality, the very thing that gave the giant his size was also the source of his greatest weakness. There is an important lesson in that for battles with all kinds of giants. The powerful and the strong are not always what they seem."*
> ***— Malcolm Gladwell***

Winning, for David, was not matching spear for spear or shield for shield. Bringing down the giant was about having the right weapon and wielding it with accuracy. Small can take on big with the right targeting, and win. Game over.

While you don't actually have a laser painting a target on your chest right now, you are being targeted all the time in an effort to separate you from your money. The most obvious example is your Facebook feed, which tries to get you to click using precision-targeted advertising. The advertiser knows that the payoff will come, not by reaching everyone, but by appealing to the most susceptible and interested.

Targeting is a big deal in the battlefield of advertising. It is the key to defeating your Goliaths. And, as I'll show in this book, it is going to be your secret weapon in generating the one source of revenue that will most effectively fuel your business: referrals.

Here's the shocker: No matter what our business or marketplace, for big brands or small, we all face the *same* Goliath.

This monster isn't hiding under the bed, it's right out there in the open, filling up the airwaves with its bluster. It's huge, and it's growing bigger every day. This massive, dominant giant can be overcome only with the skillful use of precision weapons.

What is this fearsome opponent?

It's the NOISE.

Every person we interact with is surrounded by a cloud of sensory input. Screens are everywhere. Media is a 24/7 companion. A veritable Babel of voices accompanied by a symphony of sonic stimulation makes our busy world a tough place for any of us to gain a hearing. We are doing battle with today's news, yesterday's business hassle, a chirping smartphone, tonight's dinner plans, and a thousand other distractions.

That unceasing static is what prevents people from hearing, and absorbing, our message. Noise is the primary hurdle we must overcome. We're always one click away from being ignored.

But wait — isn't our battle against competitor businesses with similar offerings? Actually, that's your smallest concern. Your true fight is not *against* other businesses, it's *for* the attention of your audience. Every potential customer is continually surrounded by the competition of unceasing voices and sights and sounds, nearly all of which is *not* from your competitors. And a lot of that noise is pretty darn interesting.

So, the Goliath of noise, overloading the senses and brains of your audience, is your main competition. In fact, your messages, too, are just part of the background noise, until you find a way to rise above it and gain that most precious commodity of all: attention. That's the necessary first step to getting the right message to the right people.

As Thomas H. Davenport and John C. Beck wrote in their book, *The Attention Economy*: "Certainly the attention economy has laws of supply and demand. The most obvious one is that as the amount of information increases, the demand for attention increases. As Herbert Simon, a Nobel prize-winning economist put it, 'What information consumes is rather obvious: It consumes the attention of its recipients. Hence a wealth of information creates a poverty of attention.'"

We live in an interconnected world of exploding information density where a million things are clamoring for our attention all the time. It's a way of life for all of us. Just think about all the distractions that derail *your* attention each hour, and you know that it's true. The statistics also bear witness to this reality.

According to Nielsen, in the first quarter of 2018, the average American spent 11 hours per day consuming non-print media — up more than an hour since 2015. And a study by Asurion concluded that the average American checks their smartphone eighty times per day. Estimates of exposure to advertising vary from 3,000 to 20,000 exposures per day. Not all of these are processed consciously, of course, but the amount of visual and auditory noise produced to try to reach each of our brains is staggering.

In fact, the average office worker gets only 11 minutes between interruptions, and it takes an average of 23 minutes for workers to get back on task after an interruption. Distractions are rampant in our work environments and exact a heavy toll on our ability to concentrate and perform.

To put it simply, people are overstimulated, overloaded, and are struggling to process the tsunami of sensory inputs that come our way every minute of every day.

Businesses trying to reach these overloaded customers fall into a common trap. To overcome the noise, they make even more noise — they shout louder! They overload their audiences with information and jargon and bullet points, instead of simple WIIFM (What's In It For Me) statements that focus on customer benefits. They are vague and indefinite about their exact offerings and their target clients. The investments we make in producing more fog and more noise are staggering, when we should really be focused on precision targeting.

Marketing consultant and educator Mark Schaefer recently coined the term "Content Shock" to describe the overwhelming amount of information that is continually multiplying online. Human beings simply do not have the time or the bandwidth to process the amount of content rushing at us.

External sources of noise are bad enough, but we each also constantly experience a swirl of interruption on the inside. Our restless minds are multitasking continuously. Like waves crashing on the shore, our thoughts, plans, and emotions collide with all that incoming input to create a constant din of distraction, eroding our ability to concentrate.

The noise is bad enough. But it's even worse than you think. We tend to carry around a delusion that people actually care about what we have to say. I hate to break it to you this bluntly, but — they don't.

Nobody cares about you, or your brand, or your company.

We're selfish. It's not you; it's me. I care about me. You're ... well, you're *irrelevant* until proven otherwise.

That sounds harsh, but it's reality. People care about themselves. Their job. Their family. Their feelings. Their future. Whatever you are offering is, at best, a means to an end. Unless you can help me feel better, do better, and reach my goals, why would I give you a nanosecond of attention?

In fact, you remain buried in the rest of the noise until you're able to demonstrate that you are fixing a pain I feel or fulfilling a desire I have. Then maybe you'll get a hearing, if you can stand out from the clutter.

The big hurdle any business has to clear to get a hearing is the WIIFM barrier. If the audience doesn't quickly find a benefit that touches them (or someone they care about), they will tune out the message as useless noise. That means that you can have the best product or service out there, but if I don't feel the value, my ears and wallet remain closed.

The buyer is always tuned in to one radio station: WIIFM. The rest is filtered out as noise.

The ability of people to *not* hear us is astonishing. In my consulting business, I have sought to communicate my value proposition — clarity wins — repetitively and simply, with blog posts, videos, newsletters, workshops, podcasts; you name it, I've pushed it out there. Yet I'll sit down with someone who has been on my mailing list for years and will commonly get this query: "So, tell me. What exactly is it that you do?" And so often, it is in that eyeball-to-eyeball human connection, explaining the value proposition, where the message finally sinks in.

Up until then, it was easy to filter me out, my message obscured behind the wall of sound. Frequently, human-to-human contact is the only thing that breaks through the noise.

The buyer is always tuned in to one radio station: WIIFM. The rest is filtered out as noise.

This filtering reality brings us to another dimension of our immense challenge. Not only are your customers surrounded by noise, not only do they perceive you as irrelevant (until proven otherwise), but *you must also overcome the flood-brain barrier.*

The human brain, as a survival mechanism, filters out the flood of input relentlessly. There are barriers to keep our brains from drowning in input. To understand this, let's briefly touch on a little-known aspect of practical brain science; one that provides the key to success for all of your sales and marketing endeavors.

The human brain is wonderfully equipped with sorting and prioritizing mechanisms to keep us sane in the midst of stimulation overload. It accomplishes this through a gatekeeper called the RAS (Reticular Activating System). The RAS consigns the vast majority of stimuli to the trash, just like an email program filtering out spam (but much, much more effectively).

The RAS is responsible for awareness, focus, and attention prioritization. Not surprisingly, it is also the conduit for fight-or-flight impulses. Every one of your customers is facing you with their RAS filter front-and-center. This marvelous piece of biological engineering is the primary hurdle in your quest to stand out, break through, and be remembered, so you have to understand what it's looking for. The RAS is attuned to focus on:

- What is new and interesting;
- What is clearly relevant;
- What is surprising, amusing, or frightening.

When you're sitting on an airplane, taxiing for takeoff, how many passenger brains do you think are tuned into to the flight attendants' messages about oxygen masks and inflatable life vests? It's all too familiar, and we don't believe it's truly relevant right now, so it becomes background chatter. Blah, blah, blah. We filter it out.

If your message is dull, undifferentiated, or difficult to comprehend, it's just static to be shunted to the trash. The RAS is attuned to grab onto that which is jarring, fresh, and clearly transmitting on the WIIFM frequency. The most effective politicians know that their audience is actually the voter's RAS, and they craft their messages to break through the noise. Forgettable is rarely electable.

This is why you need to have a differentiating message. If you are new, different, and proposing to solve a real pain or fulfill a cherished hope, you have a chance to be heard. Unfortunately, many businesses and professionals fall into the "we-do-that-too" trap of positioning themselves in the marketplace, which makes them a forgettable commodity. Moving from the status of "just another x provider" to gaining the identity as a unique go-to resource is a challenge we'll address in detail in Part 2 of this book.

The noise surrounds us. We're irrelevant until proven otherwise. The brain is filtering us. These are formidable obstacles. But we can only win if we identify the real competition in the marketplace, and in the minds and hearts of our audience. We need the right weapons for the job of breaking through and standing out. How can we overcome the resistance?

Thirteen years ago, I went into business as a consultant helping others figure out their sweet spot and branding. I learned one powerful thing about how to differentiate: The most vital positioning and marketing achievement for every individual and business is gaining *clarity*.

Clarity is getting insight into the DNA level of your individual or company makeup.

Clarity is defining what you do best for your marketplace and identifying exactly what types of clients you're seeking to serve. Clarity is being in touch with your unique differentiator(s) so that you're not just another commodity provider. Clarity is wrapping simple and memorable words around your value and your offering.

Clarity is that 20/20 focus that cuts through the fog and lets you stand out from the noise. Clarity fuels effective marketing and selling.

But clarity is more than insight. It is also the secret key that unlocks the most powerful business-building activity you can engage in: generating useful referrals.

There is an endless stream of books on selling, marketing, social media, advertising, and branding. But how to activate referrals? That's missing — even though everyone knows that the most effective and efficient way to develop business is through referrals. The best referrals are precision-targeted connections. That's how David defeats Goliath in a noise-filled marketplace.

Business success is ultimately a form of win-win matchmaking. And we put much greater stock on matches suggested by people we trust. Those trusted referrals are the quickest path to putting money in the bank.

I have built my consulting practice around helping others gain clarity, with the goal that each individual and business becomes what I like to call "referral-ready." That is, they can explain themselves so clearly, so succinctly in less than 60 seconds, that others can "get" their value proposition and know how to refer them.

Sound too good to be true? Well, based on my experience with countless business owners, consultants, and people in career transition, clarity is that one secret weapon that all of us can employ. I've repeatedly experienced the powerful impact of clarity-fueled positioning and clarity-fueled referrals in my networks.

Referral networking based on clarity is not theory for me. It's my practice, my living, and my mission.

The content of this book grew out of more than 30 years of business practice, hundreds of blog posts, and endless hours of face-to-face consulting and coaching with a wide variety of professionals and businesses. Becoming clarity-fueled is, ultimately, a liberating exercise in gaining precise focus, then crafting the fewest possible words to achieve the biggest possible impact.

If you are *seeking to gain focus, communicate effectively*, and *grow your business*, this book is for you. While I've written the clarity principles to address the needs of small-to-medium-size business, they apply just as well to brand marketers, sales organizations, career transitioners, and even teachers, speakers, and pastors. That which is true in positioning and promoting a business also carries over into all areas of life, because we're talking about skillfully using words (and, as you'll discover, word *pictures*) to effectively reach and influence people.

It's a noisy world out there and we cannot assume that people are hearing and understanding our message, let alone spreading it.

Here's what I'll be sharing with you toward that end:

In the rest of Part 1, I'll identify specific barriers to embracing your message so that you can move away from random acts of communication and toward a clarity-driven approach to making yourself heard.

Part 2 is your guide to distilling your message into key words and phrases that actually accomplish the goal: breaking through the noise and the mental barriers that prevent your message from taking root. We'll dig into the five elements of business clarity and how to arrive at a clear focus that informs both strategy and messaging.

Part 3 takes a fresh look at the power of networking through the lens of both referral-worthiness, as well as referral-readiness. Network-building is a great way to expand business opportunities if we have the right approach, including clear messaging, to equip others to recommend us.

Part 4 is about helping you design your future. As you gain clarity about your direction and message, new opportunities may open up outside of expected business models and roles. That can be both scary and exhilarating. This clarity-fueled mindset will be particularly valuable if you've always felt that you had to fit into the confining expectations of a business world designed by others.

One of the most radical concepts that you will come to embrace is the need — the *desirability* — to be "pigeonholed" in the minds of our hearers. I don't know how many times I've heard business people say, "we don't want to be pigeonholed!" I can assure you that, after reading this book, you will *strive* to be pigeonholed, and for good reason. Using clarity principles, you must design the space that you want to occupy in the mental real estate of others, which will lead to the most important result of all: business-building referrals.

I hope to take all that I've learned about clarity to help you succeed. The rest of this book will show you how to break through using succinct, vivid words that, like David's stone, allow you to go up against the giant. These distilled phrases — memory darts — are designed to light up the RAS and gain you a place in the brains of your audience. You will be understood. You will be remembered. And all of this will bring you the greatest competitive advantage of all.

You will be referral-ready.

Let's discover how to break through, stand out, and win with clarity.

CHAPTER 2

Breaking Through the Barriers

When introducing the Macintosh computer in 1984, Apple needed to grab attention with a fresh and provocative message. The result was one of the most memorable Super Bowl commercials ever created. It was daring, differentiating, and relevant (playing on themes from the book *1984*). Apple urged viewers to break out of the dull, rigid world of boring computing by adopting the modern and user-friendly Macintosh.

The Macintosh was a breakthrough product, and it exploded onto the marketplace with a breakthrough advertisement. There aren't too many ads from 1984 that people are still talking about.

That wasn't the only stroke of genius by Apple. In 1997, they unveiled the ad campaign, "Think Different." Because the compact phrase broke a grammatical rule (technically, it should be "think differently"), this unexpected twist triggered the RAS. Its brevity was suggestive and open-ended.

If you became an Apple acolyte, you could bask in the countercultural glow of being one of the elites, one of the leading-edge cool people. "Think Different" was aspirational, which made it all the more memorable.

How effective would Apple be if their tagline was, "We create microprocessor-driven products that allow our customers to do a bunch of stuff at least a little bit better than all the other platforms"? That's a forgettable, undifferentiated, boring message. Yet how many businesses have you come across that look and sound like the lockstep marching drones in the Apple 1984 commercial? If you're going to stand out, you need to take a sledgehammer to dull, commodity language.

Consider a few people and companies that have done this.

"Float like a butterfly, sting like a bee," is how famous boxer Muhammad Ali branded his fighting style. That's a word picture that's vivid, short, memorable, and quotable.

FedEx stands out by making a bold and simple statement on all of its trucks: "The World on Time." In four simple words, FedEx claims to have the broadest possible scope and promises timely delivery. "Our expedient global package delivery solutions rank high in superior efficiency" would not be so catchy or memorable.

But you don't have to be big and famous to be effective. Nate Woodruff (Instagram: @whisky_nate), as a 20-something year old, combined his passions for whisky and outdoor photography by launching @whiskywithaview, an Instagram page curating beautiful images of whisky from all around the world. Now with over 70,000 devoted followers, this creative brand-building endeavor led to a job as a brand ambassador, and to ongoing consulting work as a niche influence marketer. Initial budget: zero dollars.

(Nate is the author's son: proof positive that children do sometimes listen to parental advice!)

Angela Maiers has taken a hashtaggable phrase — #YouMatter — and turned it into a movement with an impact on thousands of students worldwide. Her message, to young and old alike: You are a genius, and the world needs your contribution. That's an upbeat, aspirational message wrapped up into two break-through-the-noise brief words.

Whatever size the business, getting attention in a crowded marketplace demands, above all, a clear and focused message: a signal that rises above the noise.

> *"If we pay a lot of money to a design agency without first clarifying our message, we might as well be holding a bullhorn up to a monkey. The only thing a potential customer will hear is noise."*
> ***— Donald Miller***

Every brand faces the same barriers to attention. We all come up against the same challenge: breaking through and becoming embedded. These barriers challenge politicians, writers, professors, and anyone else seeking to communicate to an overloaded audience.

The prescient 1976 movie "Network," made this point. It featured a newscaster who, sick of the droning dreck of network news, decides to announce that he will kill himself on-air the following week. Suddenly, listeners take interest and ratings skyrocket; the news show, which had been constantly losing in the war for attention, had broken through the noise. The network suddenly must decide whether to pull the unbalanced employee off the air or go along for the ride and watch ratings soar.

Many networks have since made their choice. The media jolt-meter keeps ratcheting higher, as each level of crazy on TV becomes the new normal.

I don't recommend shock and provocation for its own sake, but I do advocate finding a creative way to break out of the pack and stand out in a crowded field. That involves deliberately sounding different from everyone else you compete with. If you introduce yourself as "John Doe, a local banker," you're just noise. Bankers are a dime a dozen. Just another x is the worst identity from which to compete.

We've seen how the RAS filters out input that is boring or irrelevant. Now let's consider four related aspects of brain function that require us to communicate with clarity. If you're familiar with basic computer terminology, the analogies will make perfect sense:

1. Human beings have restricted attention spans (limited input).
2. Every person has only a small amount of mental space they can allocate to remembering your message or business (limited memory).
3. If the brain has to work too hard to understand, process, and remember your message, it just ... won't (limited processing power).
4. More is not better. More leads to shutdown (limited bandwidth).

Every person you're trying to reach suffers from a permanent case of GMO (Grey Matter Overload). It's not a disease; it's a hard-wired reality.

A few years ago, Microsoft released a study concluding that the average American's attention span is about 8 seconds — less than that of a goldfish. While there is no reliable way to measure human attention span, we do know that we are surrounded by an ever-growing number of options, content channels, and stimuli. We also know that we are training ourselves to be impatient with anything less than immediate results. If a website doesn't load in a few seconds, we click away to the next destination. The immediate gratification culture demands that we get to the point fast, or we'll be bypassed.

Since we now live in an extremely fast-paced environment, our rush-rush lifestyle does not encourage extended attention, let alone contemplation. We no longer have daily news. We now experience up-to-the-second news. If your message is going to get through, we have to make the best possible use of very short windows of opportunity.

If you're going to err, err on the side of simplicity. Explain using small words so that your audience is sure to understand.

As David Rock explains in his book, *Your Brain at Work*: "In Hollywood…the ideal pitch for a new movie is supposed to be so short that a studio can 'get' it in just one sentence. (There is a story that the move "Alien" was pitched as "'Jaws' in space"; the pitch uses existing elements that people know well, in high level summary form) … Simple is good. Simplest is best."

Think about the scan feature in many car radios. This function allows you to automatically breeze through the radio stations, giving you a few seconds of listening time before moving on to the next one (and bypassing all the static in the background). That's how our minds work. And, as businesses and individuals putting out a message, you want *your* station to capture attention (very quickly!) so people settle there to listen longer.

Not only must you assume that you have a very brief time to gain attention and make an impression, you also should assume that you'll be allocated a tiny amount of memory space in the overloaded and preoccupied brains of your audience. Just think about all the people you have met in the past week. If you can even recall their names and faces, how much other information have you been able to store for each individual?

I tell people in networking meetings that they should assume that they're only going to get one small slot in my memory. I can't keep them in mind for five different things. If I can comprehend and remember them for even one thing, that's a huge victory. That's what might lead to a referral.

Furthermore, you don't want to force your listeners to work at understanding your business. If it's not crystal-clear right away, why should they expend a bunch of mental energy to help you articulate what exactly you do and who you do it for? You can't expect your audience to use up precious processing power in an attempt to figure out where you stand in the marketplace. We're preoccupied with our own stuff — if listeners have to go through mental gymnastics to make it through your jargon or imprecision, that's too much to expect.

"If you say three things, you don't say anything."
— James Carville

I recently sat through a series of capabilities presentations (i.e., sales pitches) made by a group of vendors to one of my clients. In a couple cases, I could tell right away that the audience — including me — was working too hard to try to figure out the value proposition and to trace the contours of the solution. The presentations were far too general and diffuse, like a restaurant menu with too many choices. The winning provider got right to the point and provided a clear, compelling point of view. Result? A six-figure contract.

That's one of the dangers of the TMI (too-much-information) problem we alluded to earlier. More is not better when trying to cross the threshold of the listener's understanding. More is the kiss of death. An overloaded brain leads to a closed mind. A closed mind means a lost sale, and even more worrisome, spills over to lost opportunities for referrals.

In fact, you lose opportunities every time you're not clear. How many times have you walked away from a meeting with someone, perplexed about what exactly they do (or what makes them different)? How many times have people walked away from an interaction with you, failing to understand what you offer and to whom? On the other hand, if you manage to occupy the correct real estate — the right memory address — in the minds of your audience, you have tapped into the secret weapon to becoming referral-ready.

That secret weapon is *pigeonholing* yourself, using accurate and memorable hashtags.

Don't bring out the pitchforks and torches. Let me explain why a pigeonhole can be your best friend.

Here's the reality: You are going to be pigeonholed somehow, by everyone you meet. The human brain *must* sort, classify, and store. What this means is that you, your company, your brand, or your product *will* be placed in a memory slot with descriptive words and feelings reflecting the other person's perceptions.

That memory slot is your pigeonhole, and the stored bits of information describing you are your hashtags (the human brain used neurological hashtags long before users of Twitter or Instagram figured it out). Your goal is to define and occupy an accurate niche in the minds of your audience by giving them the keywords that differentiate your business. Do you want to leave that memory address to chance, or do you want to provide the correct keywords for people to understand and remember you?

How did @whiskywithaview gain such rapid growth? By deliberately joining a word picture to targeted hashtags — keywords through which whisky aficionados would find, and spread, the content of the page. Those hashtags were not random; they were carefully chosen to appeal to a specific demographic. They are the identifiers, the signposts, the badges of membership in a special club. An account called @outdoorbeverages with hashtags like #openairlibations and #sipstuffoutside would not have been nearly as effective.

Since we only have so many resources, we can't afford random acts of communication, scattering our messages like dandelion seeds carried about in the wind. The prosperity of your business depends on occupying the right mental real estate. In the human brain, the realtor's principle holds true: location, location, location.

Identifying the right memory address is critical, but, getting there and occupying your space requires two crucial communication skills: *brevity* and *vividness.*

Think about how much time you have to make an impression during a one-on-one meeting, in a sales pitch, at a trade show booth, or on a website. Seconds, right? If you have not piqued my interest and satisfied my understanding in the first minute, I start tuning out. That's why we have to turn decisively away from TMI and toward crafting words that immediately engage at the WIIFM frequency.

In fact, according to Chartbeat, a stunning 55% of visitors to media sites leave within 15 seconds. That's an awfully brief window of opportunity. And there are plenty of distractions ready to take your place if you're not immediately interesting and relevant. The websites that make one targeted point, and make it quickly, are exceedingly rare. That gives the rest of us a tremendous opportunity to employ clarity-based communications to our advantage!

Even if you can wordsmith your value proposition into a compact set of statements, you must also make it vivid. You want to light up the RAS with a short phrase and word picture that will grab attention and go directly to memory. Politicians can be masters of this: "It's the economy, stupid." "Hope and change." "Make America Great Again."

A long-winded explanation is instantly forgotten. A zippy phrase stands a chance of being remembered. Advertisers and media sites refer to this as a "hook" and use it to grab attention and provide an interesting lead-in for more information.

Author Milo Frank, in the book *How to Get Your Point Across in 30 Seconds or Less*, explains it this way: "Your deals, jobs, money, and success can all hang on first impressions. Isn't it true that with just a few words, an image is formed in your mind and in theirs, and you and they act accordingly? Often there's only time for a few words, so they had better be the right ones ...To survive and move ahead in business or in any other relationship, you must be able to get your point across swiftly and succinctly in 30 seconds or less."

Which of these two statements stands a better chance of making a lasting impression?

"We are a top-quality producer of precision-engineered micro widgets for those who have a discriminating taste in technology solutions."

"We're the Rolex of micro widgets."

One of these is a sterile statement of facts. The other is what I call a *memory* dart. Memory darts are compact, vivid, and go directly to a memory hook already existing in the mind at the desired zip code (Rolex = high-quality, exclusive, expensive). That earlier example of Muhammed Ali (float like a butterfly, sting like a bee)? A masterful memory dart.

(Memory darts, by the way, are my replacement for the tired expression "elevator pitch." No-one wants to be pitched, and most of the time when we're trying to make an impression, it's not in an elevator. Think about memory darts as your 15-second intro.)

When I chose an editor for this book, I picked Josh Bernoff because he was, in my mind, the Mercedes of book editors. (Or as he later edited it, the *Tesla* of book editors.) Does that give you a good idea of what qualities he brings to book editing?

A memory dart is your shorthand verbal business card. It is your identity implanted directly into the memory of your listener — and packaged in such a way that they can easily refer you ("Oh, you're writing a book? You need to talk to Josh, he's the Tesla of book editors!").

We can stand out. We can break through. We need to own our hashtags, identify and describe our pigeonhole, and craft our memory darts. The next section of the book will step you through the process I have developed for attaining clarity over many years, which will lead you to the pathway to being referral-ready.

A memory dart is your shorthand verbal business card. It is your identity implanted directly into the memory of your listener.

So, forget your printed business card. We need an effective, memorable verbal business card. And that is built on the foundation of your Clarity Card, which we'll discuss in detail in Part 2 of this book.

But first, we need to take full advantage of another important aspect of how the human brain functions. Let's begin with a story about fried chicken and empty pockets…

CHAPTER 3

Telling your Stories

One of the most well-known restaurants in the Nashville area is Loveless Cafe, a homey little place located west of the city. Its walls are loaded with signed pictures of famous stars who've eaten there. As a college student, I enjoyed the occasional bounty of Loveless' famous fried chicken and biscuits, so, when I moved my wife to Nashville directly after our Connecticut wedding, I wanted to introduce her to an awesome southern dinner there.

We had literally just arrived in town, without even a checking account open yet; we'd converted almost all of our cash to traveler's checks for the voyage south. For those who grew up on ATMs and PayPal, traveler's checks were like a paper version of secure payment — they could be replaced if lost or stolen, but they couldn't be redeemed without a signature. It was safer to carry them around than wads of cash.

Traveler's checks were advertised as being as good as cash, so we enjoyed our meal with cashless confidence. Until, that is, when our bill was presented, and then we were unexpectedly told that Loveless doesn't accept traveler's checks.

Uh-oh. Visions of handcuffs, or at least hours of doing dishes in the back, flashed through the humiliated mind of the gallant young groom. This was definitely going to put a damper on our relationship.

Then the waitress patted my hand and said, "That's all right, honey. You take this, and once you have your bank account set up, just send us along a check to pay for the dinner." The relief and appreciation I felt was palpable. Needless to say, I was pleasantly shocked at this very human and trusting gesture. That table server risked a few dollars one evening; the payoff was the restaurant becoming unforgettable for a lifetime.

As dozens of people will testify, since that day, I have been a raving fan of Loveless Cafe and have recommended it to countless others. In fact, my five kids are huge Loveless fans as well, so this is now a multigenerational story. And, 30-plus years later, that same spirit of southern hospitality continues to pervade the Loveless culture. To this day, we go there regularly for awesome biscuits, BBQ, and fried chicken.

Isn't that a great testimonial? And, it's one you're likely to remember if you ever visit Nashville. Because our brains love stories.

People are not hard-wired to remember PowerPoint slides or white papers. Marketing collateral often gets tossed in the trash after the briefest of glances. Long, droning presentations put listeners to sleep. If you're going to win at business, you need to put your efforts into what gets into the brain and stirs the emotions.

And that is storytelling. Stories connect us at a human level that factual statements and logical arguments can't possibly match.

This is an area where the startup or small-business owner can truly excel. We may not have a million-dollar budget for network TV ads, but we can tell our stories.

Stories connect us at a human level that factual statements and logical arguments can't possibly match.

For countless millennia, humans have passed on knowledge through stories, both oral and written. Jonathan Gottschall, author of the book *The Storytelling Animal*, says, "We are, as a species, addicted to story. Even when the body goes to sleep, the mind stays up all night, telling itself stories." Stories engage our attention and activate multiple areas of the brain.

Robert McKee, whose screenwriting lectures have influenced the makers of hundreds of hit films, writes that stories "fulfill a profound human need to grasp the patterns of living — not merely as an intellectual exercise, but within a very personal, emotional experience." Unlike sterile statements of facts, stories find an easy entrance into our minds and reach into our souls. Facts inform us; stories move us.

> *"Storytelling is the most powerful way to put ideas into the world."*
> ***— Robert McKee***

In business, we can bypass the barriers by taking advantage of the wide-open door nature has already provided for us: a hunger for stories. Being memorable and clear is so much easier when our message rides into the mind of listeners on the back of a story. Storytelling is not just for teachers and parents. It's one of our secret promotional weapons. We sell with stories. And stories are often the vehicles for person-to-person referrals.

The whisky industry sells much of its product on the basis of stories. Though some of the stories are legends of less-than-certain origin, they add to the appeal of the name brand. Go to Lynchburg, Tennessee, and you'll be surrounded by the story of Jack Daniel and how he launched his distillery near a unique spring of water. Other distilleries have generational-family stories, Prohibition stories, local-ingredient stories, unique-process stories. People aren't just buying a bottle of brown spirits. They're buying a back-story as well.

WhistlePig Distillery, one of the many recently launched craft makers of whisky, focuses its story on a dedication to rye (one of the sometimes-underappreciated grains that can be used to create whisky) and on their willingness to experiment with different barrel-finishing techniques. WhistlePig also plays up the authenticity of its Vermont farm environment, which is a "terroir" angle (the uniqueness of the physical environment and its impact on the end product). These boutique distillers often create fans through a sense of authenticity and uniqueness, which are reinforced through the company stories.

> *"We are all storytellers. We all live in a network of stories. There isn't a stronger connection between people than storytelling."*
> ***— Jimmy Neil Smith***

I urge individuals and businesses to have at least three types of stories ready to tell at a moment's notice:

1. **The evolution/origin story** — how did you get here from wherever you started? What made you choose this course, and how did you evolve along the way? And where do you envision evolving to? People want to understand how you fit in a timeline and a context.
2. **The success story** — one or more case studies that accurately summarizes how you have served a specific customer and made a tangible difference. Be sure that the example you use is relevant to the person/audience you're talking to. Listeners need to know what kind of difference you make.
3. **The how-it-felt-story** — discussing the emotional impact of something that happened. My story above about Loveless Cafe is an example. Your audience wants to hear from a human being, not an android.

If you are an individual in career transition, the exact same principles apply. Tell an evolution story through your resume/LinkedIn profile. Tell stories about how you did your best work in your sweet spot. Tell your future employer how you felt when things went well (or didn't go well) in past roles. Your career is an unfolding story, and you get to tell it in such a way that you are providing a clear signal above the noise of other job seekers who all sound the same.

My friend Thomas Clifford used to be known as Director Tom because he was a documentary video producer/director. Tom transitioned to marketing copywriting, and the common thread was this: As a video producer, Tom was a storyteller. He was gifted at interviewing and then writing up a script to tell the story via video. The only change between directing and copywriting was the medium in which Tom told business stories. He evolved while still using his core skill set.

One helpful resource for businesses that want to be more effective is StoryBrand, which promotes a framework to help companies tell their story effectively. Donald Miller, who created the StoryBrand model, has quite a story of his own — he's a guy who once weighed 400 pounds; wrote a successful book (*Blue Like Jazz*); lost everything in an ill-advised investment in a movie; then, in writing a narrative about these life events, developed a framework for effective communication called Storyline.

In time, Storyline evolved into a marketing consultancy called StoryBrand, which breaks down the narrative devices used so effectively to make Hollywood movies and shows how each business can market effectively by positioning themselves in the story of the customer. Thousands of marketers are now using the StoryBrand approach to more effectively market themselves by wrapping their message into a script that is easily understood.

When it comes to being referral-ready, stories are key, because they are easy to share. You may not remember all the facts we discussed over coffee, but one or two vivid and practical stories will embed themselves and make it much easier to pass on a referral — because the story paints the What-For Whom-Why-How-Where picture (which we'll discuss in Part 2).

"Marketing is no longer about the stuff that you make, but about the stories you tell."
— Seth Godin

Why are TED talks so popular? Because often they focus on stories. Susan Cain has created a huge enterprise focused on the value of introverts, which she launched through a very popular story-presentation. She comes up on stage with a small suitcase and explains that when she, at 9 years old, went to summer camp, her mother packed a bunch of books for her. The other campers didn't really understand — isn't summer camp all about rah-rah spirit and socializing? Susan goes on to detail what it's like to be an introvert in a world that seems to value extroversion, and why introverts have unique value to bring to the world.

Her story has influenced thousands (including me) who somehow felt defective or inferior because of an introverted makeup. It was her particular story — not just a set of facts — that moved many to feel more comfortable with their internal wiring.

Our stories tell us — and others — why we are serving in the marketplace. Bernadette Jiwa summarizes this nicely in her book *Story Driven*: "We can't see the hereditary material in our body's cells, but we know it's there. Our DNA may be invisible to the naked eye, but it manifests in the colour of our eyes and the width of our smile … Similarly, a company's DNA contains the vital information the creates its cultural identity. We may not be able to see intrinsic motivators like purpose and values or the attributes and attitudes that shape them, but … these intangibles often originate in our backstory."

Your audience is waiting for your stories. They have memory slots tailor-made to light up and remember you. Stories engage the mind and the heart. You don't want to leave that secret weapon on the shelf any longer. Especially when your customers are willing to tell their stories about you to others.

Your audience is waiting for your stories. They have memory slots tailor-made to light up and remember you.

People don't just buy stuff. People buy from people. Stories make us human, relatable, and likeable. The old adage is true: People buy from people they like. This is also true: People refer people they like. Provided, of course, they can understand what you're saying, as we'll discuss in the next chapter.

CHAPTER 4

Speaking Human

I'm going to ask for your assistance in a noble cause. Please help me understand the following statements, from one of my favorite jargon-infused websites, Blue Spoon Consulting.

> **Navigating the Transition Space to New Market Strategy**
>
> *We solve for fragmentation and continuous consumer engagement, at scale. The right way to think about a value strategy is competitively and continuously, as a stream of benefits delivered through a living system. It's not one thing that changes behavior or creates a better experience, it's many things simultaneously and interactively.*
>
> *We design 'core solutions' that fuse Chief Marketing Officer and Chief Information Officer agendas into new market visions. It's not cheap or easy to make technology upgrades flexible enough to ingest an infinite, accelerating cascade of digital applications. It's not cheap or easy to shift the center-of-gravity for brand loyalty to be based on experience, rather than functional benefits of a product. Organizational change and evolution must happen cross-functionally;*

ideally, it is change designed collaboratively with customers or partners in adjacent markets.

Using new journey-mapping software, stakeholder mapping techniques, insights drawn from original desk-side and experiential research, social media analysis, as well as our own inspiration and intuition, we develop a coherent design point for strategic transformation.

Here's a simple question for you: to whom would you refer Blue Spoon Consulting? What's the memory slot for a company that says it is "Powered by the Contradictions that Change the Game?"

Have fun storming that castle of confusion — there are at least 60 jargon-guards and a locked portcullis preventing anyone from understanding what the company offers. And no one's going to rummage around long enough to find the gate key.

Companies that approach the marketplace with a tsunami of technical verbiage can't possibly be understood, let alone referred. The RAS will reject abstract notions wrapped up in windy jargon so fast that it's oxymoronic to even think of this kind of techno-babble as marketing. It may be written in English, but it's a foreign language to anyone but the writer and maybe one guy at a think tank in Silicon Valley — and neither of those are paying customers.

Such attempts at communication are not human-ready. Many businesses fall into the trap of assuming that their audiences have the same depth of understanding, the same breadth of context as they do so, surely, they understand the message. News flash: They don't. And they won't, until you give them a well-crafted memory dart that's RAS-friendly and human-ready.

Josh Bernoff has a method he calls the "two 'huhs' technique" when someone tells him what they do. No matter what they answer, he says "I didn't quite get that. Could you say it again in a simpler way?" Then, after they attempt to simplify it, he replies with "I still didn't quite get it, could you try to explain it in a way *anybody* could understand?" At that point, they may actually come out with a simple, human-ready explanation.

The prominent Harvard psychologist Steven Pinker calls this "The Curse of Knowledge": the inherent assumptions that the reader shares the same knowledge that you have accumulated over many years. It takes work to escape the curse of knowledge. You need to remember that the reader is ignorant of what you've learned, and therefore you have to put yourself in the place of someone who doesn't know what it took you so long to learn. Until you do, you're not speaking their language.

> *"The Curse of Knowledge: a difficulty imagining what it is like for someone else not to know something that you know."*
> ***— Steven Pinker***

Here's the only safe assumption you can have as you approach the marketplace: Nobody will understand unless you make your message so crystal-clear that even family members and strangers can explain what you do. Your communications have to pass the everyday human test. It's a test you fail when website lingo or sales presentations don't get to the point in the first 30 seconds.

Consistently over the years, HubSpot has been an excellent example of using human-ready speech (and design) on their website. The site features short, straightforward phrases joined to intuitive navigation, with plenty of white space. It would be easy, in the technology marketing arena, to lead with a bunch of tech-speak, and many other companies have fallen into that very trap. It's a rare discipline to maintain simplicity over time.

Instead of simplicity, what we often get is tribal code. When my second son, who served in the US Marines Corps, gets together with his military buddies, they break into a jargon- and acronym-loaded dialect I call mil-speak. Only members of the tribe understand, but the rest of us can't follow. This happens in every specialized area — technology, education, healthcare, you name it. Most business leaders are so immersed in their own context, their own market niche, that they don't realize how ineffectively they're communicating with the rest of the world. Tribal code, or unnecessarily complex speech, closes minds.

You don't fly to another country and expect the residents to speak your language. You have to communicate with speech they understand. Winning in business involves speaking human, not spewing jargon.

One of the most insidious versions of tribal code is biz-speak — the overuse of tired business jargon to try to say … well, actually, we often have no idea what is being said. Here's an example from a website I came across recently:

> *"We partner with our clients to foster life science innovations and drive full potential of health technologies to ensure patient access to life saving medicines by identifying transformative opportunities, addressing critical challenges, and developing actionable strategies to deliver long-lasting performance in a rapidly evolving market."*

There's enough biz-speak jargon in that run-on sentence to drown an army. Here's what that website is telling us (pick one):

1. Nothing we can get our minds around.
2. Nothing we'd care to get our minds around.
3. Nothing at all.
4. All of the above.

When your language is incomprehensible, it paints no tangible pictures that the normal human being can envision. Furthermore, it relegates the company into the dreaded "just another *x*" status. For marketers, spewing jargon is a mortal sin.

Winning in business involves speaking human, not spewing jargon.

The main competitor for FedEx, UPS, is regularly guilty of wasting precious advertising real estate (the sides of thousands of trucks) by promoting jargon. "Worldwide Services" — what does that mean? It's far too general a phrase. Even worse, when their trucks proclaim, "Synchronizing the world of commerce," they're using an expression that speaks only to the tiny percentage of people working in supply chain management. For the millions of humans who see those trucks every day, it's biz-speak. Noise on wheels.

Sometimes businesses adopt these jargonized terms because they make what the company does sound more official and complex. Yet what they lose in the process, is simple, clear communication. That's a bad trade. I'd hate to live in a fully jargon-based world, where "more" is better than "clear". For example:

- Teaching = *human-generated intergenerational content transmission services*;
- Desk lamp = *location-dependent photon-generation platform*;
- Clock = *sequential time expiration presentation system (visual)*;
- Coffee = *liquified energy-resource renewal solution.*

Just for amusement, browse through LinkedIn and look at the commodity language with which people describe themselves and their roles. The biz jargon is nauseating; how many people aren't *results-driven* and *performance-oriented*? People, and businesses, make the mistake of writing for search engine optimization (SEO), as if they're going to be hired by algorithms. The only ones making business decisions these days are still humans. Settling for jargon is joining the noise parade.

I often advise businesses leaders to retain outside help with their human-ready messaging simply because we can't see our own business objectively. Since "you can't read the label of the jar you're in," gaining a third-party perspective can be crucial in translating the business value proposition into effective, human-ready language.

If you want to communicate with humans, you need to speak human.

Why is this so important? First of all, people won't buy what they don't understand. Selling and marketing activities will be labor in vain if all you're doing is adding to the existing noise. Secondly, many of your potential referrers will be regular humans who don't have the depth of domain knowledge you do, but who may very well know the customers that need your offerings. Confusing them means closing doors of opportunity for them to refer you. We'll talk more about activating these referral agents in Part 3 of this book.

For a couple years, I interacted with a gentleman (Tate Parker) at local Nashville-area networking meetings, and I had trouble wrapping my mind around his business value proposition. Cash flow insurance? What's that? Car, property, life, liability — I understood all those insurance terms. But this cash flow insurance thing was something I didn't intuitively grasp, so I couldn't make referrals.

Then one morning Tate explained it to me in very simple terms, discussing the business pains that it addressed, especially the relationship of risk to availability of ongoing/expanded credit. Suddenly the lights went on. We had crossed the chasm of complexity by arriving at distilled simplicity.

One of the most important revelations I got that morning from Tate is that many businesses are truly at risk *because their customers are at risk*. How do you mitigate that when it's out of your control? Here's how: You insure your accounts receivable. Bingo. This clear message was then embodied on his new website, which does a great job getting right to the point, fast.

Quantum Learning provides research-based sales force effectiveness tools, skills, and insights for major corporate customers, many of whom are in the life sciences vertical. The platforms are proven to move the needle despite intense competition. Instead of using jargon, however, they present their message with simple phrases (Sales Force Effectiveness Delivered); word-picture memory hooks (Lift; Moving the Needle; A-to-B Shift); and tangible data points. There is plenty of depth and technical detail below the surface, but they pay very close attention to communicating plainly and simply in all customer-facing interactions.

Speaking human is not just being simple, however; it's also a matter of projecting an authentic voice. In the book *Content Rules*, authors Ann Handley and C.C. Chapman write: "A unique, human-sounding corporate voice is critical if you want to engage, stimulate, or excite your audience — especially now, when your content is increasingly an essential mechanism through which to define, enhance, and clarify who you are. Your tone of voice, in other words, is your greatest ally: It's the basis for the relationship you hope to create with your customers."

I recently purchased some new home office furniture from Sauder. Their assembly instructions were so full of tongue-in-cheek humor, that they immediately stood out as a supplier I'd love to do business with in the future. For decades, I've put up with awfully written instructions from every sort of manufacturer. What a simple and low-cost way to make a more human experience!

So, we need to rise above the noise by speaking in clear, approachable, human-ready language. Tangibly, what does that look like for a business that wants to gain a 20/20 focus on its strategy and messaging, in words that are easy to understand? That's what we'll be examining Part 2, as we look at the five crucial elements of clarity that every business should possess.

For additional resources, including helpful forms and videos, please visit **www.claritywins.online**.

Enjoying *Clarity Wins* so far? Head on over to **www.claritywins.net**, where we make it easy for you to share highlights on your favorite social channels!

PART 2

Creating Clarity

INTRODUCTION

Choosing your Niche

Holding up a "Will work for food" sign by the side of the road does represent a fairly straightforward value exchange.

I'll do what you need (some kind of labor). You give me what I need (some form of sustenance, or the money to buy it). It's pretty non-specific; desperation can make our offering very open-ended. And, since day labor is a commodity (there are plenty of people willing to do manual work), it certainly isn't a lucrative exchange for the provider.

Desperation and open-endedness do not represent a good long-term business strategy. We need a niche and way to communicate uncommon value.

Once we get past day labor, we enter the realm of specificity. Exactly what kind of work will we do? What are we uniquely equipped to do well? What is the resulting value for the person who opens their wallet? How much effort is involved, what are the deliverables, and what are the anticipated costs?

And why should you hire me instead of a hundred other providers?

The clearest path to finding the right customers, and charging a premium for great work, is specificity. No stadium owner pays a janitor a six-figure salary, because people who do this open-ended kind of work are everywhere. But in our sports-saturated culture, a highly skilled baseball relief pitcher (especially a late-innings closer) makes a fortune for doing exacting, high-stakes work with a special set of well-honed skills.

Specific + rare + high-stakes = valuable. Generic + common + not badly needed = minimum wage. Do the math: I'm pretty confident about where you want to land when considering these equations.

Not only do we need to do this high-value work, we need to explain it. We need to be able to give simple answers to straightforward questions, if people are going to understand us.

> *"Complexity is your enemy. Any fool can make something complicated. It is hard to keep things simple."*
> ***— Richard Branson***

In this part of the book, we're going to be looking at specificity and simplicity. Your goal is to encapsulate your best strengths and your most valuable offerings into the clearest possible words that will get that message across. How do you do that?

Let's begin by asking, and attempting to answer, five simple questions that will lead you to your clear value proposition.

CHAPTER 5

The Five Elements of Clarity

If you know even a little bit about journalism, you know that there are a handful of core questions that every reporter is expected to ask and answer: Who, What, Where, When, and Why. You're even better off if you can also answer "How."

Your story is incomplete without answering these fundamental questions. But that's the case, not only with journalism but also with your business. In fact, these are the very questions that lead you to a 20/20 strategic focus — a clear business direction. That's why I use the following format as a summary whenever I do clarity consulting:

- **What:** Single-sentence summary of exactly what product or service your business provides.
- **For whom:** Succinct but detailed description of the ideal client who needs what you have to offer.
- **Why:** The key business realities — the business needs, pains, or hopes — that will trigger a decision to listen and buy.
- **How:** The "superpower" possessed by your business that differentiates you in the marketplace.

- **Where:** The domain(s) and/or location(s) where you do business with clients.

The purpose of arriving at these clarity statements is to set your business compass to true north, so that you are providing the right solutions to the right customers for the right reasons. Clarity provides the road map (or, if you prefer, is your GPS) to guide you to your professional destination. You are defining what you do best, because you will always do your best work in your "sweet spot."

Why do so many companies fail to set their GPS properly? I think one reason is that people are afraid to actually close doors, to say "no" to potential business. Clarity is an act of courage to say "yes" to the best business and therefore to decisively say "no" to work that isn't a good fit. It is a public declaration of confidence.

Another reason for failing to have a clear road map is laziness. I don't have a cure for that. The market does, though. It's called a "Going Out Of Business Sale."

Clarity is an act of courage to say "yes" to the best business — and therefore to decisively say "no" to work that isn't a good fit.

If your GPS needs to be set (or reset), it may well be because no one ever gave you a tool to help you set it. So, here's the formula: These five statements are what will guide you into sketching out that sweet spot and choosing your direction. Let's take a closer look at each of these clarity elements:

Start with ***what***. Every business aims to provide a product or service that somebody will find valuable enough to exchange money for. When I ask what someone does for work, my experience has been that very few can articulate their offerings in a concise manner, before the attention-span-clock runs out in 15 seconds or so.

Here's the typical answer you may get: "I'm a marketing consultant." "I'm involved in financial services." "I work in sales with XYZ healthcare company." "Our company, DroneZone, takes surveys using drones."

While these may be factual answers, they are nowhere close to providing the listener with an accurate picture of the precise business needs that you address.

Think about the price tag attached to this failure. That first impression is the moment of truth, the singular opportunity to either gain someone's ear (and potentially a sale or a referral) or lose their attention. It is no exaggeration to say that a clear *what* is the most important business development tool that you have. Since so few craft an effective summary of their business, it is a fantastic opportunity for you to stand out from the crowd.

Let's take our friend from DroneZone. This would be a much more effective response: "The use of drones for aerial imaging is booming, and DroneZone works with real-estate agents and city planners to quickly get 360-degree photos and videos of their locations."

This more detailed single-sentence summary paints a picture in the mind of the listener of what exactly the service is and who it is for. The wording elicits further questions. Furthermore, it's an expression of the company strategy, its reason for being: Drones are replacing helicopters and other more expensive methods for a wide variety of needs, and DroneZone has identified two of the hottest areas (real estate and city planning) in which to plant its flag. Because this offering is new, and interesting, and specific, DroneZone Guy gets through the RAS and wins a slot in my memory. Also, because it sounds so cool, I want to learn more.

Now, behind that statement is a series of strategic decisions — DroneZone had to decide how it would do imaging, how extensive that imaging would be, how to package the offering, and who was the lowest-hanging-fruit clientele in their situation. The what element means deliberating about where the company can position itself competitively, not as a commodity, but as something special.

Your *what* isn't just woodworking or IT security services. Those are categories, not specific offerings. Categories are the main filing cabinet. Now you need to tell us the specific drawer, and the correct hanging folder, if we're to know the precise information necessary to buy (or refer). Arriving at a clear what statement involves eliminating a whole host of other possible choices, so there can be clear focus on the best service for the most willing (and needy) customer.

Strategically, every business needs to make that ideal customer decision — the ***for whom***. There are more than 7.4 billion people on planet earth, and the vast majority of them are not your customer. And so, you must paint a detailed portrait of your best potential client — I use the term "bullseye customer," instead of the more general phrase "target market." You need to clearly define that bullseye customer in your own mind — and in the minds of your sales representatives, your marketers, and your partners. Your goal is to plant that picture in the minds of anyone who can potentially refer you.

Will you be serving small or large businesses? What industry? What is the typical title and role of the person who needs your service and has budget authority? What department are they in? What are the professional challenges they are probably experiencing right now? What emotional state might they may be in due to those challenges? Who might be other influencers in deciding on your offering?

The beauty of making the bullseye client decision is that it immediately informs a whole set of other decisions about how and how not to advertise, market, and sell. You can take time and money that would be wasted chasing after a less focused (and less lucrative) target market and channel it instead into a highly targeted communications and referral strategy.

Brains on Fire, a creative marketing agency in Greenville, South Carolina, paints the portrait of its ideal client in terms of *purpose*:

> *"We typically work with nonprofits, associations, foundations and socially conscious for-profits and startups who view people as more than a transaction and their business as a catalyst for positive social good. We help our clients succeed through a mix of participative insight, insanely clear strategy, emotional storytelling, soulful identity development and authentic community building. If you want to grow your organization by doing good, bringing people together and contributing to the world in a meaningful way, let's talk."*

Circling back to DroneZone Guy — by clearly defining who he wants to serve, he can now make a simple, targeted inquiry to fuel referrals: "Do you know any real estate agents that are looking for a competitive edge?" They don't want referrals to the 64-year old traditionalist just running out the clock until retirement. Their bullseye client is probably younger, hungry to grow aggressively, and on the leading edge of technology.

The *for whom* decision is also relevant for those in career transition. There are countless companies out there to consider working with. Which type of company specifically needs your skill set and experience? One growing pharma company I knew had pulled together a bunch of people through various acquisitions, and as a result its training department needed to be totally restructured. A friend of mine whose skill set was structure building (department organization, curriculum design, culture) was the perfect fit for the job, and he took a department that had essentially no form or direction and turned it into a cohesive, influential unit that quickly gained the notice of the C-suite. A couple years later, he was handed a global role to replicate his success.

Intertwined with the *what* and the *for whom* is the ***why*** — the business need that calls out for our solution. Organizational consultant and author Simon Sinek has recently put a spotlight on the importance of knowing your *why* (Google his TEDx talk on the topic). What is the marketplace need that makes me/my company necessary? Why are we in business, and what tangible impact are we seeking to make? Company leaders that know their *why* tend to speak with much greater conviction than those whose purpose is simply to go on existing.

Launching and growing a business is not done in a vacuum. You can't just hang out a shingle and expect customers to show up with suitcases full of money. And the *why* isn't some fluffy sentiment, like "we want to make the world a better place." Your *why* has to address a business pain that people actually feel (we are experiencing 35% annual employee turnover), a business need they are experiencing (we have to grow sales by 10% or we go bankrupt), or a business aspiration (we're going to restructure our software support team so that we're the very best in the industry). These are the pressing motivations that open minds and wallets.

"We offer corporate training solutions" does not speak to the *why*. But this does: "Our two-week on-boarding training framework increases new hire satisfaction by 35% and reduces one-year turnover of new hires by 50%." Now we're talking about numbers that matter. Bottom-line results. Reputation enhancement. Success.

If DroneZone Guy can present some statistics and case studies showing how real estate agents using his services moved property faster, then the *why* becomes a no-brainer.

Of course, every company is going to make claims as to why a client should work with them, and, most of the time, it sounds like everyone is playing the same song on repeat: "We help you achieve corporate mission imperatives by translating strategy into tactics that address KPIs blah, blah, blah." I'm not sure how many company websites are interchangeable with their competitors — just swap out the logo and a few words, and it's all the same drivel — but I've seen a whole lot of carbon copy marketing going on where businesses simply don't differentiate from the crowd. When you blend in, like a bunch of penguin clones on an ice floe, nobody remembers your name.

That's why every business needs a ***how*** — some unique capability, some special domain knowledge, some peculiar framework or product or service or connection that rises above the rest of the marketplace. Business advisor Chris Brogan calls this your "superpower," and it's just as relevant for individuals as it is for companies. Individuals should try to build their career direction around their superpower, and companies should also identify what they are uniquely great at and approach the marketplace with that message front and center.

Most companies can do multiple things, but the key is to distill your message and offering down to something special and uncommon. One training company I've worked with provided a suite of solutions and services that sounded pretty much like every other provider in that marketplace, but they excelled at big, messy, longer-term projects that required a lot of personnel and project management. When they partnered with a client, they provided needed *bandwidth* to get the big, complicated jobs done. That was their superpower. They could tell multiple success stories and hammer home the point: Call us for your major challenges.

That particular company also had another point of differentiation — the ability to tackle global projects. And that is the ***where***; the slice(s) of the marketplace where you can add value. When we talk about your *where*, we are considering more than one dimension. The most obvious is geographical — are you providing products or services locally, regionally, nationally, or globally? Where are your customers physically located? FedEx might deliver the world on time, but your business may only serve a few local zip codes.

But your *where* also involves the market sectors you serve. I like to portray this in several dimensions: vertical domain (such as automotive, healthcare, or hospitality); horizontal function (such as HR, manufacturing, or sales); and company size (from nano to huge). Mapping out your specific *where* allows you to narrowly focus your promotional message and outreach efforts. (We'll discuss this in more detail in chapter 9.)

Apple, you may recall, at first concentrated on two major sectors of the marketplace for Macintosh (education and creatives). Only after they achieved deep penetration in a few targeted realms, and then developed broader offerings, did they cross over into the general marketplace.

Companies that provide solutions for regulatory compliance often need to choose one or two specific target markets, and perhaps only one country, because the tangle of regulations is so specific in each niche. Their customers will typically be found in specific departments (legal, compliance, medical affairs, or training, for example). Those in complex industries, such as nuclear power, will have far more complicated needs than, say, a small local chain of auto repair shops.

Your goal is to define the realm in which you do your best work, where clients most love you, and concentrate on niche success. Dominating one *where* is what can enable you (if desired) to expand into other realms.

Your goal is to define the realm in which you do your best work, where clients most love you, and concentrate on niche success.

DroneZone doesn't have a totally unique advantage (others can use drones), nor will they be the only ones serving real estate and city planning. But by being first-movers and building up a portfolio of case studies and deep bench of experience, they can establish a dominant position — a concept we'll explore more deeply in chapter 16.

Distill each of these five elements of clarity down to one or two very brief sentences, so that your employees, your customers, your advocates, and your prospects can easily digest and understand exactly where your value lies. These simple phrases need to be "human-ready" — that is, a normal human being not necessarily immersed in the jargon of your particular marketplace can easily understand how you're positioned and who you serve. That's why I use a format called a Clarity Card to enforce simplicity and create well-targeted referrals. For example, here is the Clarity Card for my consulting business:

Steve Woodruff, Clarity Consultant	
WHAT:	Steve helps businesses and individuals gain fresh focus and direction, and distills their primary value proposition to a succinct and memorable message.
For WHOM:	Steve advises sales professionals, small businesses, consultants, and people in career transition who want the clarity that makes them more "referral-ready."
WHY:	Until you can describe your value proposition succinctly, you'll find it hard to rise above the marketplace noise and get sales and referrals that will grow your business.
HOW:	Steve helps clients define their sweet spot, determine new opportunities, and design clear messaging - all in less than a day. Because, *"you can't read the label of the jar you're in."*
WHERE:	Steve works with companies and business professionals through the United States and Canada.
Contact: steve@stevewoodruff.com	
	www.clarity.cards

The Clarity Card format proactively paints the picture in the mind of the recipient of what a great referral would be, in all five dimensions. It's your sweet spot, your pigeonhole. It is also a handy summary of your corporate strategy, a touchstone for current and future decisions about direction.

How do we arrive at clear direction, strategy, and wording about these five foundational pillars of our business? That's what we'll cover in the rest of Part 2.

CHAPTER 6

Getting in your Zone

I'm fascinated with DNA. The more scientists dig into it, the more complex and amazing they find it to be. DNA is the internal genetic programming that shapes who you are and what you do. It's the "nature" half of the ongoing nature versus nurture discussion of human development.

DNA is also the term I use to describe what a person should focus on as the first step toward business clarity. You need to understand the internal wiring, the unique strengths, the makeup that determines what drives you. No matter how much passion and desire you may have to be a football linebacker, if your DNA has determined that you're five-foot-eight, medium of build, and speedy as an armadillo — well, nature has determined that you qualify to be in the stands, cheering, not on the field getting run over.

On the other hand, if your makeup involves being highly analytical, creative, curious, and driven to solve problems, you might be a great consultant. Some things can't be learned or forced; they're in the wiring. Recognizing your strengths and capabilities — sequencing, so to speak, your personal and professional DNA — is what helps you choose the most fulfilling direction and allows you to do your best work. As Terry Orlick describes in his book In *Pursuit of Excellence*, you want to labor in your *zone of excellence.*

Another book that had a transformative effect on me earlier in my career was *Now, Discover Your Strengths* by Marcus Buckingham and Donald O. Clifton. Taking the StrengthsFinder assessment from the book helped me gain clarity on what I could and should do best — and why. Whatever path I took, I'd excel best if the endeavor involved strategic thinking, intellectual analysis, creative inquiry, and disciplined responsibility. Sure enough, as I looked back on all my professional and volunteer roles, it was in those places of strength where I always flourished. A 20/20 view of our strengths makes it much easier to map out a future toward living and working in our zone of excellence.

Buckingham and Clifton's assessment also liberated me from concentrating on overcoming my weaknesses and seeking to be a competent professional in areas that didn't fit my DNA. I was never going to love spreadsheets, or social schmoozing, or repetitive tasks, or repairing engines. No wonder I hated that one summer job working in a plastics factory!

What is true of individuals is also true, to a large degree, of companies. It is true that businesses are not hard-wired the way humans are — by changing personnel, adding fresh capabilities, and evolving into new markets, companies and brands can morph considerably. But most companies start out, and if all goes well, continue in their own zone of excellence. For the sake of chasing short-term revenue, however, many business leaders get distracted and start grasping at work that really isn't a great fit for them. That's a zone violation.

"Our DNA is as a consumer company — for that individual customer who's voting thumbs up or thumbs down. That's who we think about. And we think that our job is to take responsibility for the complete user experience."
— Steve Jobs

The DNA of Walmart has always been making a lot of basic stuff available, at the lowest possible price. Period. You would never expect to find exclusive, high-priced fashion accessories there. The Walmart ecosystem is not built for that type of product, that type of sale, that type of buyer. Shampoo? Yes. Dom Perignon Champagne? Zone violation.

Earlier in this book, I mentioned UPS when talking about (in)effective messaging. But while UPS may not articulate well what makes it great, if you look closely, you see that its DNA as a company is *operational excellence*. The extent to which the people of UPS study logistics and process, and seek to create efficiencies, is remarkable. Do you know why UPS trucks almost never turn left? It's all about maximizing safety and efficiency. Saving time and money, and preventing accidents, is part of their success formula.

Operations, yes. But not leading-edge fashion. Nobody's going to the prom in a UPS uniform.

Speaking of those three letters, in a slightly different order: You need to have a USP (Unique Selling Proposition). Every company needs to articulate their sweet spot. As John Michael Morgan says in *Brand Against the Machine*, "Your USP is focused on something you do that no one else offers. It also must be a strong benefit to the customer. 'In business since 1923' … doesn't say that you're the best. It just says that you're old."

Here's an example of what happens when you don't pay attention to your DNA. A software company I worked with for a decade had a great platform for delivering online assessments. Because the core client base was almost entirely made up of commercial training departments in the pharmaceutical sector, we decided to go after the development of custom eLearning — also known as online training — as well. This was a potentially lucrative adjacent offering that would expand our business with our existing clients. Even though our deliverables were quite good, we weren't able to succeed for several reasons:

1. Our core development personnel were software system (platform) designers, not content creators. We now had to hire and manage a very different set of personnel.
2. The development and sales cycles were entirely different, involving project-based work (one-time development) versus licensed platform support (annual maintenance and usage fees).
3. We tried to expand from being a dominant and unique supplier in our well-defined niche (online assessment), to competing with dozens of other companies who already had an established track record in online training. We went from dominant provider to "just another" player, entering the commodity zone where there was already lots of noise.
4. We tried to re-architect an established brand in the minds of our customer base, which sounds easy in theory, but is very difficult to pull off.

We had obscured our USP. Eventually, we scaled back and returned to our core competencies, leading to greater stability and profitability, and eventual acquisition by a larger platform company.

Knowing what you do best is what helps you decide what to say "yes" to. Oftentimes, it's your customers who are telling you what they value most from you. They may have the clearest view of your sweet spot, and they vote with their dollars.

Mark Schaefer advocates for a very simple two-word test: "Only I … " (in the case of a company, it can be "Only we … ") The goal is to fill out that sentence by pinpointing what is the special capability and offering you bring to the table: something that others can't easily replicate. This is often going to be driven from the DNA level — a deep individual or company competency.

On the other side of the coin, one of the greatest benefits a company can gain from identifying its sweet spot is the ability to say "no" to distractions dressed up as opportunities. Some client and project opportunities look very tempting, and the siren song of a major chunk of revenue can be very loud in your ears. But once you venture outside of your zone of excellence you risk doing substandard work (or work that takes twice as much effort for the same pay) and damaging your reputation.

You should not respond, "As you wish!" to every customer request. Some pieces of business turn you south instead of north, essentially paying you to move in the wrong direction.

Not all business is good business, and not every customer is a good customer.

That's not to say that companies can't stretch their capabilities and offerings into new or adjacent areas. That can be a very successful strategy. But if businesses aren't 20/20 focused on what the core competencies are, and haven't identified the best opportunities aligned with those competencies, they can easily lose their way and impede real progress.

I love the TV show "Shark Tank," which reveals this point in detail. Some of the most pointed grilling you'll see there happens when the experienced panel of entrepreneurs questions a guest on their plan to move out of their company's zone of excellence. Time and again, the sharks warn business people about the dangers of unproven models and ill-considered expansions that seem like a questionable fit. Also, not surprisingly, one of the most common reasons given by individual sharks for not making a particular investment is that the business being proposed is not a fit for *their* sweet spot.

When considering business direction and opportunities, you can use a rubric like this to guide your choices. Is this work/this client:

1. *In line with your big-picture goals?*
2. *Profitable?*
3. *Enjoyable?*
4. *In the zone of your strengths?*
5. *Scalable and/or reproducible (can you expand, or re-use, what is being developed)?*

The more positive the answers, the better the fit. But if the answers are negative, you may perceive red stop lights or yellow caution lights as you move into a business direction without a clear enough sense of your core DNA. You should be saying, "No, this will be a distraction, not an opportunity."

The poster child in the Internet era for incoherent business direction is Yahoo. Seemingly without clear design or focus, Yahoo acquired a mismatched set of online assets and tried to somehow patch them all together into … well, nobody knew what the endpoint of all the acquisitions was. The company, and the various properties it acquired, floundered. There didn't seem to be any clear road map to success.

Jeff Goins is a best-selling author of five books (so far). As a young marketing director and soon-to-be-father, he had a conversation with a friend. This is how Jeff recounts it:

> *"What's your dream?" (my friend) asked.*
>
> *I was 27 years old at the time and "over" dreams. That was kids' stuff. I was now an adult — a married man with a mortgage, steady job as a marketing director, and plans of a baby on the way.*
>
> *"I don't have one," I said.*
>
> *"Hmmm, that's interesting. Because I would've said your dream was to be a writer."*
>
> *Oh. Yeah. That.*
>
> *"Well," I said, "I guess I'd like to be a writer … someday. But that'll never happen."*
>
> *Paul paused for a moment before he spoke again: "Jeff, you don't have to want to be a writer. You are a writer. You just have to write."*
>
> *As activist and author Parker Palmer wrote, "Before I can tell my life what I want to do with it, I have to listen to my life telling me who I am." And my life was telling me that I was a writer.*

Jeff's DNA was loud and clear. Write. And now he has built a seven-figure platform as an author encouraging others to write their stories.

How do you come to a clear-eyed statement of your professional DNA? Here's the key point: The signposts are always in your past work. Which clients really loved your work, and why? Which projects did you seem to excel on, filled with energy and purpose? Where have you stood out from the competition? What is your point of differentiation? What do you really want to do, and can you turn that into something valuable and sustainable?

As Mad-Eye Moody said to Harry in *Harry Potter and the Goblet of Fire*:

> *"Play to your strengths."*
>
> *"I haven't got any," said Harry, before he could stop himself.*
>
> *"Excuse me," growled Moody, "you've got strengths if I say you've got them. Think now. What are you best at?"*

Your track record and your customers generally provide you with the best clues about your real strengths. When I've consulted with companies about gaining focus, one of the first things I do is ask about case studies. That's the primary clarity data pool. When they tell great case study stories, their eyes light up, their volume rises, and their heart beats faster. If that happens to you, that's how you can tell that you're describing your zone of excellence. The negative experiences in your track record provide clarity by contrast — that past situation didn't work out so well, because I was doing this (not in my DNA) instead of *that*, where I could have truly excelled.

Chris Ducker begins his book, *Rise of the Youpreneur*, with this idea: "One of the biggest mistakes I see entrepreneurs make is that they never figure out how to define their business. This can make it almost impossible to build a successful brand and, consequently, a profitable business over the long term. Becoming a Youpreneur means you won't make that mistake … [k]nowing who you are will enable you to truly captivate your audience."

You have a choice to gently prune your second- or third-best work to hit the target, which requires a well-defined destination.

As we'll show in the next chapter, now you need to sketch out your customers, or more specifically, your bullseye customers.

CHAPTER 7
Identifying your Bullseye Customer

My son, in his time as a Marine, became an excellent rifle marksman. Floating around somewhere on the Internet is a video of him hitting a target from a mile away — on his first shot! There's nothing random about precision targeting. You'll never find a sharpshooter that's shooting wildly into the air, hoping that some target somewhere will get hit. Precision wins, not randomness.

That's true in business as well.

As John Michael Morgan says in *Brand Against the Machine*: "You can't focus on your target audience until you define them. Your target audience is the group of people most likely to purchase from you and those you are in the best position to serve. All your marketing efforts should be directed at these people."

Yet, in your mind and in the minds of those who know you, the situation, location, and identity of your target customer (or, as I prefer to call it, your *bullseye* customer) is often poorly defined. And that's a problem — how can you focus your efforts to reach a target that you're not seeing clearly; and, how can someone else aim a referral your way when they don't know what kind of customers you help?

Aim at nothing, as the saying goes, and you'll hit it every time.

"The aim of marketing is to know and understand the customer so well the product or service fits him and sells itself."
— Peter Drucker

Businesses can spend far too much time taking random shots and hoping for a hit. Often, promotional efforts are much too unfocused to succeed.

For instance, many marketers obsessively focus on the size of their email list or on the number of followers they have on social media. The more contacts, the better, regardless of how diverse and potentially inappropriate for your services they may be. If you send a message to 10,000 people, you might hit one or two that are feeling a need. But are they the right people, seeing the right message? And in the process of hitting those few, you've wasted time and effort on 9,998 people that are not a fit for what you're selling.

I understand that selling is, in part, a numbers game. But we can always be more intelligent in our targeting.

When a fisherman wants to catch widemouthed bass for a meal, he does not zip around random bodies of water in a boat, throwing chum in the water and hoping to snare a fish on some trailing hooks. He goes to where the bass are — a quiet corner of the lake, where there is aquatic vegetation — and he uses the right kind of lure to attract his customer. Or, in this case, his dinner.

If someone sends me a mailer for fractional private jet ownership, or for spa treatments, they clearly haven't done their homework. A local BBQ festival? Now I'm in the bullseye!

You can fix this targeting problem for your business. Fortunately, it's a lot easier than you might think. It's not about greater reach with a general message, because more isn't necessarily better. It's a matter of targeted reach with a precise message. Five warm buyers are better than 10,000 cold prospects any day of the week.

Here's the goal: You want to paint word pictures of your ideal customers in the minds of your listeners — after first clearly defining them in *your* mind.

Five warm buyers are better than 10,000 cold prospects any day of the week.

Compare these two statements:

"We provide digital marketing solutions to healthcare companies."

"We partner with marketing directors in emerging medical device companies who are overwhelmed with all the choices of digital platforms and need long-term, strategic guidance to build a digital marketing approach."

The first statement may be true, but it's vague. It tells me nothing about the client who is feeling the business need that is being addressed. No one sees themselves in that description — and no one is likely to respond to it.

The second statement paints a very specific picture that includes the type and size of customer the provider does their best work for, the level of the decision-maker, the emotional state they are probably experiencing, and the type of business relationship that you are proposing (long-term strategic partner, not a one-and-done project shop). Anyone who fits that description will say "Ah, that's me. These guys are there to help *me*."

The vague description goes immediately into the mental trash can. But the detailed portrait might lead you to think of a colleague you knew from a prior company who now has that exact role and is feeling the overwhelming angst of navigating through the digital marketing world.

You can call this strategic narrowing. You're always going to be serving a subset of every human being on planet Earth. Why leave that bullseye subset vague and undefined?

While your company may do a few different types of work, with some variations in the client demographic, what you want to do for your salespeople and referral advocates is to paint a singular picture that is your bullseye — the ideal sweet-spot customer. Why? Because you've decided that this is the type of engagement that will be most profitable, enjoyable, successful, and potentially scalable for your business. I call this my 85% rule: Promote the one sweet spot you want to be most known for and keep the other 15% in your back pocket for situations where someone might be able to use you for your additional offering.

Think about how this brings disciplined focus to your efforts. In the example above, should the sales and marketing staff for the digital provider put a lot of effort into pursuing large, established medical device companies? (No; the smaller/emerging companies are better prospects). Should they go after adjacent neighboring sectors, such as pharmaceutical companies? (Probably not; the marketing approach is very different). Are they looking to set up meetings with managers or CEOs? (No; it's people at the director level that make this decision.) Are they creating some custom app for a client? (No; they won't do this unless there is a clear pathway to more long-term, consultative work.) And … who might they partner with for joint business opportunities? (Other companies serving the same type of customer.)

Suddenly, the picture comes into focus. You've sketched the center of your target, so you aim the bulk of your business development effort there. And if you've chosen wisely, you'll realize that there can be an awful lot of money waiting for you in your newly narrowed target group. You don't need a million customers. You just want to secure a limited number of the *right* ones.

Some might say that broader is better — cast as wide a net as possible. More bait in more places leads to more fish — right? It's math! This sounds appealing on the surface, until you recognize that now you're expending a lot of time and effort untangling more lines and reeling in the wrong kind of fish. Plus, you're more likely to end up in the eel-infested waters of vicious competition.

A broader focus with a more diverse audience requires more effort, yields a lower response rate, invites more competition, and undermines a targeted referral approach. The broader your focus and message, the more you risk becoming a commodity.

By painting the picture of your ideal customer, you have informed your marketing approach, simplified your sales process, and given your clients, partners, employees, and friends a precise target for referrals. You've sketched the bullseye for them.

> *"There is only one winning strategy. It is to carefully define the target market and direct a superior offering to that target market."*
> ***— Philip Kotler***

The carmaker Volvo has always touted the safety features of their vehicles. Safety: Who is that appealing to? Hormone-filled teens? Men in midlife crisis? No; their bullseye audience is not looking to win a drag race, they're trying to protect their kids. Volvo knows that there's plenty of money in that demographic slice, and it's a customer type that will always be replenished. Volvo doesn't have to design a car (or message) that appeals to everyone, just to their core audience.

A while back the research company Forrester, engaged in a fight with much bigger Gartner, embarked on a role-based strategy. Each research group would serve only customers in a specific role, such as CMOs, interactive marketers, CIOs, or directors of information security. The narrower focus enabled it to continue to grow despite the presence of a much larger company dominating their target market.

For whom did author Chris Guillebeau write the book *The $100 Startup*? Are the bullseye customers budding entrepreneurs or corporate ladder-climbers? The subtitle says it all: "Reinvent the way you make a living, do what you love, and create a new future." And the audience is clearly not the venture-capital startup crowd. Chris is aiming at the regular person who wants to bootstrap themselves into a new model of business and life: the restless creative. Chris himself managed to create a lifestyle business that enabled him to visit every country in the world (193) between 2002 and 2013, while maintaining the hugely successful blog, "The Art of Non-Conformity," which he calls: "[A] home for remarkable people of all kinds. If you've ever felt like there must be more to life, this site is for you."

There are countless niche customer groups; one is surely right for you. For instance, I focus a lot of my clarity consulting efforts on very small businesses — solo consultants, contractors, entrepreneurs, and leaders of small but growing startups. That audience desperately needs help in finding new ways to grow, and that's where I make the most impact. Even though my clarity principles can help a larger company, too, I don't seek referrals into huge companies like Procter & Gamble, where the procurement process may take many months and the management overhead could kill me. I want to help the people and companies who are left behind when it comes to branding needs.

Business strategy expert Brian Moran advises his large corporate clients that serve the SMB (small-to-medium size business) sector not to think of that group as one uniform customer type, requiring one message, but to stratify intelligently. For instance, entrepreneurs who are scaling up are looking to buy in order to grow quickly; existing businesses may view the same investments more as expenses requiring a different justification. The subgroups require different positioning and messaging.

The owner of a niche woodworking company told me that almost every one of his current customers (the decision-drivers) were women in their 40's or 50's. This immediately suggested a focused referral strategy. Because his work focuses on high-end craftsmanship, we decided that one of his top social media strategies should be to take before/during/after pictures and give them to his customers so that they can brag about their updated home projects with friends on Facebook or Pinterest.

His demographic, equipped with visuals, would do most of the selling for him on platforms where their online friends already liked to share. He didn't need to expend a lot of effort trying to gain a wide following on Twitter or Instagram.

When sketching your customer portrait, it's important to remember one other principle: *You don't have to do business with people you don't like*. Some customers are very high maintenance; they demand much and give little in return. Somehow, there's always far more pain than gain. One aspect of your bullseye customer could be spelled out in phrases like this: "I don't work with jerks."

People often think in terms of hiring and firing suppliers. You should be thinking in terms of hiring and firing customers.

Here are some questions to ask yourself as you sketch out your bullseye customer:

- With what customer type(s) do you have a track record of success?
- Which customers (titles/roles/names) actually have the money to spend and the authority to make spending decisions for the services you offer?
- What are these people feeling right now (frustration, confusion, fear, being overwhelmed, hope, greed)?
- Do you have the right medicine to fix the pain(s) or meet the desires they acutely feel?

- Do you already have customer (or referral) advocates who can speak to the needs of your bullseye customer type?
- If you have identified a target market, is there a precise subgroup within that target that actually better represents your bullseye?

Some group of customers out there desperately wants what you have to offer. They're the ones you need to reach; you aren't looking to persuade the millions of others that aren't a fit. The time you spend creating your bullseye customer portrait will save you an immense amount of time and effort trying to cast a wide net without clear aim.

Your ideal customers want you and what you uniquely offer. Once you reach them, you get to deploy your superpower in serving them, as I describe in the next chapter.

CHAPTER 8

Finding your Superpower

If you follow any kind of sports, one of the great privileges you get is to see an athlete with superpowers.

Clearly, anyone who reaches a professional level in sports is immensely talented. For instance, there is not a single player on an NBA team that doesn't have exceptional basketball skills. But then there are phenoms like Steph Curry, who can hit 3-point shots like no one you've ever seen before. If his coach told him that the best way he could help his team was to concentrate solely on defense — or worse, to warm the bench for half of each game so that lesser players could take their shots — that would be an utter waste of talent.

Any team has its best chance of winning by deploying its superpower.

Your superpower is *how* you excel — what makes you (or your business/team) stand out among a sea of other providers. You can call it magic, or secret sauce, or value-adding differentiator — however you label it, it's your strategic advantage. Your DNA, talent base, knowledge, and experience provide the raw material for a professional superpower, a point of greatness.

So, what is your business *doing* (and how is it doing it) that is remarkable?

I have found that most individuals and companies are not aware of their superpower, because they're so used to what they excel at, they simply take it for granted. I don't know how many times I've said to people as we've brainstormed their business together, "do you realize how rare and exceptional that capability is?" Sometimes the biggest challenge is identifying and embracing for ourselves what is already there.

To win, you have to be clear about your superpower, and you need to make that differentiation clear to your customers. Otherwise, you remain part of the noise.

Big companies can have superpowers. Netflix won the video delivery race by building on convenient, rapid gratification (once streaming took hold, *rapid* became *instant*). Blockbuster offered the same movies but didn't adapt to home delivery, digital access, and device ubiquity. A passel of physical brick-and-mortar outlets was no longer a winning formula.

To win, you have to be clear about your superpower, and you need to make that differentiation clear to your customers. Otherwise, you remain part of the noise.

Apple's superpower? Making technology user-friendly and beautiful. Walmart? Low prices, fueled by constantly improving efficiency (volume purchasing and robust supply-chain). McDonald's? Consistency; wherever you go, the food is the same. The Jenner/Kardashian clan? Fame exploitation (really — they're quite good at it).

Other organizations thrive by building on their unique superpowers. The nonprofit Habitat for Humanity specializes not just in building shelters (anyone can do that), but in activating volunteerism and local involvement. Blood:Water takes a similar approach — partnering closely with communities — to catalyze change in African countries impacted by the water and HIV/AIDS crises. The differentiator in these two cases is not the size of a check being written; it's long-term, strategic thinking, joined to mobilization.

Even big cities can have superpowers. I moved to the Nashville area, not because it was Music City (an excellent and accurate memory dart, by the way), but because the middle Tennessee area is suffused with a culture of human welcoming, creativity, and collaboration. I hear it all the time: "Even the cashiers are friendly here!" I'm not alone in appreciating the Nashville blend of opportunity and hospitality; as of 2018, one hundred people per day are moving into the greater metro area. (Lower taxes and a mild climate are, of course, a nice bonus!)

Individuals also have superpowers. At a trade show one day, a lady from another company approached me; she was curious about our company's offerings. Within minutes, I was completely captivated by her magnetic warmth. I've met a million salespeople, some of whom were very effective, but never before had I witnessed the instant rapport that this woman so naturally created with others. I invested two years convincing her to join my team, and whenever we'd go out on sales calls, I'd just stand back in awe and watch the magic happen.

My wife's superpower is an uncanny ability to organize … anything. Everything. All the time. In fact, I've hashedtagged her #Combobulator (yes, there is an opposite to "discombobulation"). It's the one-word summary of how her wiring is manifested in action.

For decades, Amica was the best insurance company that no one had ever heard of. In fact, for the longest time, they did not advertise at all; their only growth strategy was through person-to-person recommendations from current policyholders. Amica always topped the A.M. Best insurance company ratings, because their superpower was *unusually prompt, personal, dedicated customer service.* This engendered fanatical devotion from customers; and, of course, spurred steady growth by referrals. I can speak out of personal experience that this led to multigenerational loyalty from customers.

It's not just big companies and individuals that can get in touch with their superpowers. For small and micro businesses, it's absolutely crucial to position yourself in the marketplace according to your standout capabilities. You can't possibly compete with the scale of larger companies, but you absolutely can carve out a niche with focused excellence. When you stand out from a crowded field of providers, you gain the opportunity to take residence in a memorable pigeonhole in the minds of others.

"You're either remarkable or invisible. Make a choice."
— Seth Godin

Why is author Seth Godin so popular with readers? In two words: *pithy insight*. Many others have written on marketing topics, but few with the out-of-the-box thinking summarized in easy-to-digest phrases that Godin uses. If he wrote long-winded tomes on business theory, he'd be just another unknown author buried on a shelf somewhere. But his blog, his books, and his speeches are all marked by his unique ability to deliver bursts of enlightenment in accessible, vivid words. Not many individuals could take the concept of a purple cow and embed it into the thinking of hundreds of thousands of businesspeople worldwide.

The purple cow concept is all about being remarkable, as a way to stand out in the marketplace. Being remarkable will only happen when you rise above commodity level and excel in your unique abilities. No one raves about e-commerce these days, or about deliveries by the U.S. Post Office. But Amazon — with Prime, Kindle, same-day delivery, and other advances — always stays top of mind. Everything you need, easy, quick as lightning; that's how Amazon differentiates.

How can individuals and companies determine their superpower? One of the simplest ways is to ask this question: *Who loves you, baby?* In other words, what do your customers rave about? What kind of work are you doing that gets the best feedback? When people turn away from competitors and turn to you, why is that? Sometimes customers are the best compass as you set our strategic direction; they'll tell us what we're great at, if we think to ask.

Here are some superpowers I've come across over the years. You can undoubtedly add to the list:

- Personalized, one-on-one service
- Team motivation
- Fashion sense
- Empathy/EQ (emotional quotient)
- Listening skills
- Verbal/written fluency
- Rapid responsiveness
- Future vision/innovative thinking
- Speed of development
- Athleticism
- Hand/eye coordination
- Pattern matching
- Analysis
- Infrastructure/systems design
- Consistency/dependability
- Thorough, detailed project management
- Operational excellence
- Collaboration/group facilitation
- Outstanding quality
- Creative, beautiful design
- Customization
- Deep domain/industry knowledge
- Business acumen
- Broad, value-adding connections
- Digital wizardry
- Content development/curation

A business can be good at several things, but there will be one aspect that truly stands out. That's what you want to identify and promote. Besides asking your customers directly, here's one method you can use to identify your superpower:

1. List out five to ten of your projects/client relationships that were (or still are) success stories.
2. Pull out of each of those case studies just one or two things you did exceptionally well, things that the client clearly valued. Maybe the client told you that that's why they chose you or why they plan to continue choosing you.
3. Look for the commonalities in those success stories. You'll begin to see themes emerge.
4. Talk to several trusted friends, colleagues, or customers and ask for validation: "It seems like I do my best work when I'm doing this, what do you think?"
5. Scan your closest three to five competitors and see how they stack up against your superpower. Are you unique? Can you define yourself for bullseye customers in a unique and different way in your messaging?

Another method I find helpful is to identify the "enemy" that your customer is facing. Superpowers are always deployed against bad guys! The bad guy may be a big competitor, but often, it's actually more related to the environment or circumstances ("the digital world is confusing and fast-moving — we serve as your trusted guide so that your decisions turn into long-term wins instead of short-term boondoggles.") When you hear multiple clients complain about the same thing, you've found your bad guy. How are you going to rescue the client from the clutches of a malevolent enemy?

One boutique training agency I worked with truly stood out on the creativity front, particularly for live training events like product launches. They had a remarkable capacity for thinking up new angles. The bullseye client referral for them wasn't the conservative plodder; it was the risk-taker who had a taste for new and different, who wanted out-of-the-box thinking with a creative edge.

A business can be good at several things, but there will be one aspect that truly stands out. That's what you want to identify and promote.

My own superpower is creative synthesizing. I happen to be skilled at analyzing disparate thoughts and ideas, distilling them to core themes, and then articulating and applying them in the real world. That ability sheds light on everything I've ever done, in every role, all the way back to my college psychology papers at Vanderbilt. It's DNA-fueled magic. In fact, "magic" is what operating in your superpower feels like, even if you're not bursting out of a phone booth wearing a red cape.

Unfortunately, that realization about my superpower didn't come to me 30 years ago by opening up a fortune cookie ("Tomorrow you will be a huge success through creative synthesis! 24-8-33-7-15"). I realized it by occupying different roles, being willing to experiment (and fail), and getting feedback about what was of most value to others.

According to Robert Steven Kaplan, author of *What You're Really Meant To Do*: "It's vital to reflect on situations in which you were at your best ... many of us have a hard time remembering [them]. We can get so caught up in the day-to-day pressures and obligations of our jobs that we forget about those situations in which we were absolutely fabulous. Recalling these situations is critical because you can gain insight from them that can help guide your actions today."

Can you summarize your superpower (as an individual or as a business) in one or two keywords? Go ahead and hashtag yourself! Those words can provide the light with which you navigate the entire course of your professional life — because doing what you do best is how you'll become outstanding.

We don't create happy customers and use our superpowers in a vacuum. Every company operates within a certain sphere — a market*place*. Now it's time to consider where you can most successfully plant your flag: the specific niche where your ideal customers live and work and open their wallets.

CHAPTER 9

Defining your Niche

Imagine moving into a new town. As you drive down Main Street, you spot a storefront emblazoned with a sign that reads: NOW SPECIALIZING IN EVERYTHING!

Would you rapidly pull into the parking lot, thanking your lucky stars that you found retail nirvana — the one place where you can fix your car, cut your hair, buy your electronics, and get a medium-rare Kobe steak?

I don't think so. But you might bestow the Oxymoronic Business of the Year award on such an institution. What could be more contradictory than "specialize" and "everything"?

No business does everything, for everybody, everywhere. If it tries, it will do many things badly. No individual seeks to do every job, for every company. "Consultant in whatever you need" is a prescription for poor performance.

Jack of all trades, master of none — that's a certain recipe for being a forgettable commodity. There is always the temptation to say yes to whatever a client might ask for and to cast the broadest possible net for potential clients.

Every-thinking puts you on a path to nowhere. Niche-thinking channels your efforts in a productive direction.

"We provide IT support and services," a tech company might proclaim on its website. To whom? Where? This type of company is now competing with everyone from IBM to the 17-year-old in his parent's basement.

Every-thinking puts you on a path to nowhere. Niche-thinking channels your efforts in a productive direction.

"I don't want to be pigeonholed!" is what I've heard from many business leaders and from many individuals in career transition. But, as I've shown, your clients are compelled to put you in some kind of memory slot. You want to choose that best niche in which they can file you and easily find you.

For example, I love coffee. Dark, strong, quality coffee. Probably I love it a little bit too much, if we're being honest.

So, when I'm on the road, do I pick up a cup of hot liquid from just any old storefront? No. My default is Starbucks, because they occupy that niche in my mind. Peet's will do nicely when on the West Coast, and I won't turn down Dunkin' Dark Roast in New England. I've pigeonholed these companies, so I can get what I want while I navigate a complex world.

In the memories of others, you must have an address where you are found. It needs to be the right niche, corresponding to your marketplace sweet spot. In fact, your ultimate goal should be to occupy the "go-to provider" label for your niche. Defining your niche is where clarity comes in.

Michael Port, in his well-known volume *Book Yourself Solid*, talks about becoming a category authority. Besides creating credibility and trust among your target clients, he points out that this also allows you to earn higher fees, because you stand out from the masses.

Defining Your Marketplace Niche: A Four-Dimensional Approach

Practically speaking, how can a company (or individual) gain a clear focus on its specific niche? You can't paint the picture for others if you're not clear on it yourself. So, let's look at four niche-defining dimensions that help you articulate your place in the business world:

- **Vertical Industry** (e.g., education, auto manufacturing, healthcare, energy, financial services, or consumer products).
- **Functional Domain** (e.g., sales, marketing, human resources, manufacturing, or compliance.
- **Physical Location** (local, regional, national, global, virtual).
- **Customer Profile** (company size, title/role of buyer).

Consider these, put together, as your business coordinates, the marketplace sweet spot *where you do your best work for your best customers*. Scattering attention across too many marketplaces is like tossing seeds to the wind, instead of carefully cultivating a productive garden.

The more focused you are in as many of these four dimensions as possible, the easier it is for you, and others, to identify your best prospects for new business development. Let's take a closer look at each of these dimensions.

Vertical Industry

Your company may well have some kind of specialized *vertical industry expertise* that your clients value: deep experience and a confident level of familiarity with certain types of businesses or intellectual property. That vertical is where both you and your bullseye customers live, and breathe, and spend. To successfully serve clients that reside in a specialized vertical (and to acquire their respect), you need to be thoroughly immersed in that narrow industry: its terminology, its processes, its challenges, its history, and its key players.

A high-tech semiconductor manufacturer isn't looking for production advice from Frank the Neighborhood Welder. Frank doesn't "do" silicon. Boeing isn't going to consider an advertising agency with a passion for the consumer fashion marketplace, because a provider in touch with the latest Hollywood or youth trends isn't going to advance their business. That's a vertical mismatch.

These companies, and hundreds of thousands of others in various verticals, need specialized suppliers.

If your business is providing specialized services in one or several verticals, that will require some level of expertise. Since your business is probably not capable of serving all verticals equally, where do you have the most expertise, and which vertical is most profitable and has the most growth potential? As you specialize and become known as an expert, you're likely to serve some verticals better than others.

If your sweet spot has a vertical focus, that means you're saying no (or should be!) to a hundred other vertical markets. A major component of clarity is declaring a decisive yes to one niche that implies a forthright *no* to a bunch of other marketplaces.

There's plenty of money in every vertical. Focus on where you have the best chance of earning it.

Functional Domain

Every company that is past the startup stage begins to separate into functional areas, often identified with departmental labels. The marketing department has a very different set of needs and goals than, say, the manufacturing group. Manufacturing leaders are looking for help with efficiency, quality, safety, and compliance, while the marketers need customer research, segmentation, competitive intelligence, and promotional creativity.

As an example, pharmaceutical companies typically include functional domains like R&D, Clinical Research, Manufacturing, Operations, Finance, and Commercial. Subdomains on the commercial side may include Sales, Marketing, Sales Operations, and Training. Each of these functional domains has its own distinct universe of specialized vendor/providers.

You can't possibly be good at providing multiple offerings for disparate audiences; that abandonment of focus is a sure recipe for failure. You must identify the functional domain where you do your best work, and where there is the greatest need.

Many times, a business that serves corporate clients will have a functional expertise (e.g., compliance) joined to a vertical industry (e.g., financial services). Other times, there may be a functional expertise (outsourced IT support) that spans multiple vertical industries.

If my accounting firm asked if they should expand into video production, I'd be inclined to advise against it. Competence in one domain does not mean effectiveness in another. At last check, number-crunching skill sets don't typically translate into visual creativity and storytelling.

In the universe of functional areas, your business needs to have a specific focus to sharpen your sales approach and cultivate targeted referrals. Can you articulate for others the departmental or functional sweet spot that you serve? I might know a grey-suited drone in Finance at Ford Motor Company in Detroit, but he is not a referral target once I know that you need to speak with a decision-maker in the Global Operations Excellence group for Asia.

Speaking of cities like Detroit, we also have a third dimension to consider: physical location. Where does your niche sit geographically?

Physical Location

Many years ago, all business was local, but not anymore. Some local businesses still succeed best where physical proximity is at the forefront — a coffee shop, a restaurant, a dog-walking service. The customer base is either nearby, or physically passing through. Neighbor-to-neighbor referrals are still primary in these cases.

An application like Yelp is very useful for rating businesses in specific geographical areas. This became evident to me recently when staying at a resort in Cancun; the employees had been trained to encourage guests to leave reviews (positive, of course!) on Yelp. Why? Because their bullseye customer was seeking to know about the customer experience at a resort in a physical location that they were considering for a visit.

But we also live in a networked global economy, which opens up whole new opportunities from around the block or from around the world. Graphic designers, web programmers, writers, editors, virtual assistants: All of these specialized services, and a host of others, can now be performed without physical proximity.

When I recently relaunched one of my websites, the graphic designer was local in Tennessee, the web programmer was in Romania, and the site was hosted in Alabama. Physical location was totally irrelevant. The only thing that mattered was competency, and the path to finding suppliers was trusted referrals that crossed geographical borders.

The words *marketplace, workplace,* and *customer* can now mean just about anything when it comes to location. Therefore, we have to define them, whether geographically or not, for our business.

What about your business? Are you serving only local clients? Regional? National? Global? Does geography even matter for your client base, or can you serve them virtually? You'll need to consider different approaches and messages depending on the geographical scope of your business and the location of your bullseye customers. Those who might refer you need to be able to recognize where your customers will be found.

Geographical focus may or may not be central to the strategy. For example, Lee Company is a very successful regional home and facilities services provider focused on Alabama and Middle Tennessee. Their maintenance trucks are ubiquitous in the area, and they advertise heavily in their geographical target marketplace. But outside of the region, they're basically unknown. They've identified the boundaries of their sweet spot, and they're happy to be a big fish in a well-defined, smaller pond. They're not advertising, selling, or seeking referrals in New England.

If you're providing commodity-level services that are the same across customer types (say, landscape maintenance or window installation), you may not need vertical industry or functional domain expertise. Grass is grass, glass is glass. You can help a technology company just as well as a bank. The competitive edge for you is providing great customer service.

Whatever your business model is, you need to be able to articulate the physical "address" of where you do your work — or why it doesn't matter. And, while describing the location of your niche, you also want to give people a sketch of the type of customer you are seeking to serve.

Customer Profile

When you draw up your profile of the ideal customer, you should be thinking of these three elements:

- Company size
- Company culture
- Title/role of decision-makers

Long experience has shown me that not every size client is a good fit for every size provider. Often, we're tempted to think that we want that big "whale" client, but for a solo consultant or micro business, that can often lead to disaster. For instance, such a client may demand 90% of your time and provide the bulk of your income, but what happens if there is a change in that client's management or direction? We've all seen advertising agencies take huge hits because of over-dependence on a top client that decides to take their business elsewhere.

Large client companies can often have an arduous procurement process, and many times are slow to pay. Both of these factors can cripple a small provider. Therefore, you need to realistically assess whether you can do your best, and most profitable, work with micro, small, medium, or large clients, or divisions of a larger company.

An interior designer may do fabulous work one-on-one with individual wealthy clients but be utterly unable to scale up to a large corporate project. It's not a matter of talent; it's a mismatch of size. Every business needs to know its capacity and bandwidth.

During the initial Internet boom, I watched as one smallish, successful digital learning firm with a narrow focus and good track record suddenly tried to scale up into a major digital platform/marketing company. Venture-capital fueled visions of getting to the big leagues led to a hiring binge and ambitious offerings aimed at whole new levels of clientele. As with so many unrealistic business models during the tech boom, this was followed by a crash-and-burn contraction all the way back to the size of the original company. The brass ring that the big clients and huge contracts represented remained out of their reach. They wrong-sized themselves for a wrong-sized target marketplace.

Evaluating what size client provides the most profitable work can spare you from many bad decisions that would lead to chasing after revenue from customers that are a bad fit.

Understand that not all clients have the same attitude or culture. If you've been in business for any length of time, you know what I mean when I refer to a high-maintenance client. Never satisfied, they always want more, taxing your resources to the point where the work is unprofitable, and the environment is uncomfortable.

Specialize to the point where you can fire them.

I've walked away from some potentially lucrative customers because I know (through my own interactions or through the input of others) that they will be miserable to work for. I remember meeting with one top-five pharmaceutical company where, after an uncomfortable interrogation (I thought it was going to be a nice get-to-know-you meeting — silly me!), I was informed that *if* our firm was selected to work with Megacorp, it was expected that we would treat them as if they were our *only* client.

I walked out and didn't look back. We had lots of other clients and prospects without that attitude. Why enslave yourself to a petulant giant?

Really, not every company is a good match. Some are too fast-paced, some are too plodding, some are always nickel-and-diming, some are afflicted with founder-itis (a company leader who can't let go and micromanages everything).

You should be able to tell others about your positive client experiences and paint the picture of what made those customers ideal to work with. Why? Because that way you, and people who provide referrals for you, can be on the lookout for the right kind of match.

We had several flooring providers come to our home recently. One of them was quite business-like: factual, formal, transactional. That company might have been capable of doing a great job, but I wasn't in a robot-hiring mood for this job. The next guy was warm, comfortable in his own skin, and asked great questions. The prices came in close, but the decision was an easy one. The real human won.

Client relationships are still relationships. Seek to work with people you like.

Finally, your customer profile should be detailed enough that you can give others information such as the customer's role, and even a specific title. Some of the solo consultants I've networked with have indicated that, because their targets are relatively small businesses, they almost always end up selling directly to the owner of the company. That's good to know, for the sake of crafting the message (business owners have their own specific needs and pains), and for making an accurate referral. On the other hand, in a larger company with an extensive hierarchy, buying decisions relating to your offering may be made at the Director or Manager level. When you network with other professionals and tell your success stories, be sure to include a portrait of the type of decision-maker you typically work with.

Putting this all together, your strategy is to find your bullseye customer within your niche marketplace. Know which industry the customer works in. Know what department, too. Identify the geography. And focus in on the type of firm you serve, such as startups, sole proprietors, medium-size businesses, or large companies.

It might be a mistake to narrow the aperture in all four dimensions. Maybe you want to serve companies across the whole United States. Or perhaps you serve three main verticals. That's fine; you can leave those dimensions a little loose.

But unless you focus down in at least two, and preferably three, of these dimensions, you will be too unspecialized to generate targeted referrals.

> *"We are turning from a mass market back into a niche nation, defined not now by our geography but by our interests."*
> — ***Chris Anderson***

Now that we've defined our niche marketplace, let's move on to another vital element to generating business success — defining and packaging our go-to-market offerings.

CHAPTER 10

Designing your Offerings

Nobody buys things that don't fit. Or, if they do, they're not satisfied.

I have wide feet. Triple-E width. Narrower shoes hurt, and I certainly don't enjoy investing money for ongoing pain. There aren't that many companies that design their shoes for feet like mine. Skechers does, though, so that's where I look first. I don't care how cool your brand is, or how awesome your shoes look, if they don't fit, I don't open my wallet.

Furthermore, nobody buys what they don't understand. If your company offers end-to-end scalable business platform middleware integration solutions, then I really have no idea what you're offering me. Or what you're offering others to whom I might be able to refer you. That's a lot of lost opportunity.

What we offer needs to be a clear and obvious fit for our customers.

Every business has important decisions to make about go-to-market offerings. Given your bullseye customer, and your specific niche in the marketplace, what kind of transaction are you going to propose? The key concept is *packaging*: What are the deliverables that your customers want and can understand, and what words will you wrap around them?

It's not enough to say that you provide something. You need to help others envision exactly what they're buying — in concrete terms.

What we offer needs to be a clear and obvious fit for our customers.

Your offering needs to have a (literal or figurative) shape, size, quantity, timeframe, cost, and outcome. It needs some kind of tangible outline that allows the customer to picture the work relationship and transaction. If what you are offering is vague or unclear, customers won't buy. They have to understand what it is — its benefits and particulars — and it has to feel like a fit for their need and their budget.

A cup of coffee for $2.25 is a pretty clear exchange. But when a company says that it provides scalable business growth consulting engagements, then I really don't know what the transaction is. Let alone the WIIFM.

"We empower your employees to leverage their full potential" is excrement wrapped in a blanket of fog. Tell people what they're buying — in words that have real meaning.

What are some common forms of offerings? Here's a small sample list:

- A product (or family of products)
- A subscription
- An experience
- A one-time service
- An ongoing service
- Outsourced service(s)
- A customized solution
- Specific knowledge/content
- An application
- Advice (coaching, consulting, therapy)
- Strategy/planning
- Promotion/communications
- Diagnosis
- Instruction/training
- Labor
- Maintenance/repair
- Staffing
- Matchmaking
- Distribution/delivery
- Quality control/testing

This list could go on and on, but there is one phrase you should have at the forefront of your mind as your craft your offering (and the message to promote it):

People buy tangibles.

If you approached me and said, "I need to up my marketing game," and I replied, "Sure, engaging me to help with that costs

$25,000," with no further explanation, that would definitely register as a No Sale. I haven't described the outline of the bang you're going to get for the buck.

This is where *packaging* comes in.

Whatever it is that you provide, you want to be able to express it as a differentiated, results-producing, clearly defined package.

- **Differentiated.** Why would I buy what you are offering compared with other providers?
- **Results-producing.** How are you going to relieve my pain and/or make me successful?
- **Clearly defined.** What exactly does your offering include and not include? Is there a clear deliverable?
- **Package.** Help me envision the exchange in tangible terms.

Example: Let's say Sheldon is a professional business coach. That's a more "squishy" and esoteric offering than, say, a cup of coffee. And there are a ton of business coaches floating around. So Sheldon has to "thingify" his offerings: Turn what he does into tangibles with deliverables, labels, templates, and levels.

To differentiate and make his services easier to envision and buy, Sheldon might package himself this way:

- **Differentiation:** Based on years of experience, he coaches small-business owners who are wearing too many hats and feel "stuck." Sheldon knows a specific market segment and understands their business pain.
- **Results:** He provides concrete strategies to more effectively manage your staff so that within three months, you

reclaim at least one day a week for higher-level strategic leadership. There is a promised, measurable outcome.

- **Clearly defined:** He spends a half-day up front doing discovery and diagnosis with you and draws up the result in his "Peak Revenue A-to-B Action Plan" (deliverable). He then schedules 90-minute weekly coaching calls to work together on implementation, during the initial 3-month engagement (clear and limited expectations/ commitment).
- **Package:** Sheldon also provides a "Gold-level Concierge Service" for unlimited support calls and for 6- or 9-month coaching engagements (using common imagery to explain differing levels of service).

Even better — Sheldon packages his entire approach with the name "Unstuck Business Accelerator," which uses his *5-step Framework for Rapid Revenue* workbook. The customer is now buying concrete things that have labels. If they can envision it, then they can assign value to it and intelligently decide whether to buy it.

How much, how long, how many, how often: These quantifiable elements give people a better idea of the actual exchange. Windy and vague generalities that the customer can't understand are an invitation to say, "No." The more concretely we can describe the offering, the more comfortable our customers will feel about going forward.

Your safest assumption is always this: Potential customers or referral advocates will *not* immediately or intuitively understand what you offer. You live and breathe your stuff, and you think you'll just say it and they'll get it — but they don't. Making the complex simple is the key to opening wallets.

Restaurant menus do this all the time. This meal includes *x*, but *y* and *z* are extra; You can upgrade your order to x+ by paying this amount more. We are trained to make decisions based on lists, levels, and labels.

Douglas Karr, a marketing technology expert based in Indianapolis, once packaged his work as customized consulting engagements. His offering wasn't differentiated; the results were not quantified; the nature of the engagement wasn't clearly defined; and there weren't any packages for potential clients to envision and choose from. As a result, he had a difficult time explaining what he did for customers; everything was a one-off, and therefore, revenue was not recurring.

With uneven work, he struggled to keep employees productively engaged. Then, he moved to a model of packaged monthly retained services, with a specific list of tangible services provided, and outcomes promised. Streamlining the offerings into a scalable and repeatable model, he was able to shed employees in favor of using contractors, and now only needs a handful of repeat clients to keep the revenue faucet flowing. Bonus: He wastes very little time and effort on business development, so he can focus on doing great work and cultivating referrals.

If there are different levels of service, I often recommend the Gold-Silver-Bronze packaging concept so that people have choices. People more intuitively understand how tiered levels of pricing and service correlate. Also, here's a hint: It can be a very smart idea to package a low-price, low-commitment starter offering for new clients. Create some kind of small, bite-size deliverable for the customer that needs to gain a comfort level with you as a provider. It's easier to make a $50,000 decision on something big if the customer has already tried out a $5,000 door-opener successfully.

Consultants sometimes offer a one-hour fixed-price call, a simple, limited transaction to help both the buyer and the seller understand if the relationship is a good "match." This can then evolve into a one-time consulting gig, a monthly retained coaching relationship, or some other packaged set of services that are a win-win for both parties.

Sometimes the packaging is the differentiator. Fifteen other companies may provide something similar, but if you discover a way to offer it that makes the decision easier, that may be all it takes to dominate. Netflix packaged movies as downloads, and absolutely buried Blockbuster. Zappos turned shoe-buying into a pleasant, buy-and-try-from-home experience, instead of the miserable store-hopping ordeal it's always been.

Vacation resorts offer a lot of similar amenities, experiences, and prices. But what is the particular appeal of an all-inclusive resort (pay one price, and everything is included)? Simply put: The packaging means that I don't have to think about pulling out my wallet for anything, freeing me from decision-making dilemmas. Vacations are meant to be liberating experiences, and this approach greatly increases the relaxation factor.

Packaging is an especially important exercise for consultants and other solution providers. I saw one provider give this one-sentence summary of his work: *"I help clients identify problems, develop a solution and create the vehicle to resolve it."* Huh? What is he selling here, an all-purpose magic wand? Totally intangible.

You want what you offer to be clear and obvious. Remove as many barriers to understanding and purchase as possible. Simple sells. Confusion doesn't.

Now, to address a pet peeve. I wish I had 10 dollars for every company that advertised itself as providing "solutions," because I'd be a very rich man. The overuse of the word *solutions* in our business vocabulary is a mortal sin because it's so often used as a sophisticated version of the word *stuff*. "We don't really know exactly how to explain what we do, so we'll leave it open-ended and call it solutions." Jargon-terms like "solutions" are the opposite of clear and obvious. If you've got that generic word in your business name or tagline, you'll need to get specific about just what it is that you're solving with your "solutions." Otherwise, it's fog with a side of vagueness.

People want to say yes, feel good about the exchange, boast to others about what they bought, and move on. Good packaging makes that happen.

Your Clarity Card is, in essence, your business packaging. It provides the clear and simple answers to that moment-of-truth question that every professional faces on a regular basis: "So, what do you do?" It is the summary of who you and what you offer. In verbal or written format, you can share it with others, and they will know what value you provide and how to refer you.

Once you've achieved clarity on your *what, for whom, why, how*, and *where*, you are far better equipped to sell and to seek referrals. Having a clear focus and message makes you referral-ready; now, you need to pro-actively cultivate your advocates who can send targeted business your way. I call this *referral networking*, and that's what we'll cover in Part 3.

For additional resources, including helpful forms and videos, please visit **www.claritywins.online**.

Enjoying *Clarity Wins* so far? Head on over to **www.claritywins.net**, where we make it easy for you to share highlights on your favorite social channels!

PART 3

Referral Networking

INTRODUCTION

Activating your Referral Agents

Everyone who has been in business for more than 5 minutes understands that referrals are the most powerful way to get new business.

According to Forrester Research, 80% of all B2C and B2B purchases include some form of WOM (word of mouth) recommendation during the purchase cycle. According to Nielsen, 84% of Internet users worldwide trust recommendations from people they know — a greater level of trust than any other form of advertising. And a Harris poll found that the vast majority (more than 80%) of Americans seek recommendations when making a purchase of any kind.

Here's how McKinsey summarized it (McKinsey Quarterly, April 2010): "Consumers have always valued opinions expressed directly to them. Marketers may spend millions of dollars on elaborately conceived advertising campaigns, yet often what really makes up a consumer's mind is not only simple but also free: a word-of-mouth recommendation from a trusted source. As consumers overwhelmed by product choices tune out the ever-growing barrage of traditional marketing, word of mouth cuts through the noise quickly and effectively."

The warmth of human relationships turns a referral into the best advertising vehicle ever. If a sales person or an advertisement says it, our skeptical shields are up. If a customer or trusted friend says it, we listen with a far more open mind.

Mark Zuckerberg put it this way: "People influence people. Nothing influences people more than a recommendation from a trusted friend. A trusted referral influences people more than the best broadcast message. A trusted referral is the Holy Grail of advertising."

I am convinced that the greatest (and least utilized) weapon in our arsenal for business success is referrals. And referrals happen when we intentionally and effectively network with others. That's a practice I call referral networking — a proactive, personal, and purposeful approach to cultivating people and turning them into advocates. And it all starts with being not only referral-ready, but also referral-*worthy*.

CHAPTER 11

Be Referral-worthy

If you're going to use referral networking as a growth strategy, start with this question:

Should anyone refer you?

If your company is not doing a good job with customers, or if your ethics are dubious, or if you are just another commodity provider, your business is likely to fail (and deservedly so). This book can't help you if you're not worthy of a recommendation.

Just put the book down and concentrate on making your business better. Clarity only works when there's a clear and accurate description of how your business is excellent.

If a business or individual is not *competent*, is not *conspicuous*, is not *considerate*, and does not win the *confidence* of others, then the best outcome for all involved is removal from the marketplace gene pool. Let's take that apart.

Competence is table stakes in this game of business. To put it simply, your company is competent when it is capable of performing the tasks and responsibilities it takes on. You have found what you're good at, and customers come to you because you get the job done right, nearly all of the time. This is why it is so critical to identify your professional DNA. You have to find your unique strengths and build up a track record of great work in situations that are a good fit for you.

If you're sloppy, tardy, or just not skilled enough, you cannot expect existing clients to help you gain new customers to disappoint. A bad reputation earns anti-referrals, and bad news spreads very fast in any marketplace.

On the other hand, everybody loves referring providers that they know will excel in their sweet spot, because both they and the client gain outstanding value from the connection. A few years back one company I work with created an excellent selling skills program. The company earned six-figure contracts with a top pharmaceutical company because I recommended them for their niche competency.

> *"Do what you do so well that they will want to see it again and bring their friends."*
> — ***Walt Disney***

"Yeah, they were okay, I guess ... " is not much of a referral. A lukewarm recommendation because you were not conspicuously better than competitors is hardly a ringing endorsement. Business and individuals earn referrals by being remarkable, not ordinary. Commodity-level products or services do not earn word-of-mouth business.

We win by exceeding expectations, having a great attitude, and making the entire user experience a positive one. There's a very clear reason why Chick-fil-A has created such fanatical devotion among their customers. It's because they train their employees to be extraordinarily polite and helpful, in every customer interaction. Nobody raves about ordinary (or poor) customer service at other chain restaurants. Not surprisingly, Chick-fil-A is the top-rated fast-food restaurant for customer satisfaction in America, and they generate more revenue per restaurant than any of their competitors.

Remarkable gets talked about. Ordinary gets ignored.

"Quit or be exceptional. Average is for losers."
— Seth Godin

People refer businesses, but often, they are really referring individuals. And the people who most often earn referrals are, above all, *considerate* — kindness and likability are always in fashion when it comes to business. Winners at life and business know that caring about others is an immensely powerful way to generate goodwill and create loyalty.

Bob Burg, along with co-author John David Mann, has written a series of books on this theme (using the phrase "Go-Giver"). His successful writing and speaking career embody the Go-Giver principle — kindness and consideration ooze from his pores with every online and offline interaction.

"Your influence is determined by how abundantly you place other people's interests first."
— Bob Burg and John David Mann

Put competence, conspicuousness, and consideration together, and you're building the most vital business asset of all: trust. We want to have confidence in the people and companies we do business with. We seek to deal with ethical people of character, not with sharks. In fact, the most precious thing you can develop over years of work is a reputation of trustworthiness. Trust is hard-won, easily lost, and springs from a foundation of principle and character.

Trust is the currency of referrals. Trusted people win the word-of-mouth battle of business development every time. If you've earned the trust of people I already trust, their referral of you to me is worth more than any other form of marketing.

If you've earned the trust of people I already trust, their referral of you to me is worth more than any other form of marketing.

Word-of-mouth marketing is the fastest route to success. Jay Baer and Daniel Lemin, in their book *Talk Triggers*, underscore several reasons:

1. It is *hyper-relevant*. The recommender customizes the recommendation to fit the receiver's perceived needs. No other form of marketing is as personalized, and consumers increasingly desire personalization.
2. Positive word of mouth *saves the recipient time* by giving him or her a referral and recommendation, eliminating some or all of the research needed to make a sound decision.

3. When offered by consumers to one another, word of mouth is *independent*, as the talker has no financial interest in the sale of the service. A consumer's independence adds credibility and persuasiveness to the recommendation. This trust advantage is the key to why word of mouth is so crucial today. Fundamentally, we trust businesses and organizations less than ever, and we trust people more than ever.

Having a "talk trigger" — some remarkable differentiator that people gladly talk about with others — is a fabulous short cut to gain exposure without the expense of advertising. Jay and Daniel cite Doubletree Hotels' delicious chocolate chip cookies as an example. Sure enough, in one of my very first marketing blog posts, way back in 2006, I also wrote about Doubletree and their cookies.

When Marcus Sheridan wanted to revitalize a lagging swimming pool company, he went about earning trust in a remarkable manner, by providing an extraordinary amount of online information, more than any competitors were willing to reveal. In his book, *They Ask You Answer*, Sheridan states: "The irony is that every industry has hundreds of buyer-based questions … As consumers, we expect to be fed great information. As businesses, we like to talk about ourselves and therefore don't focus on what our prospects and customers are thinking about, worrying about, and asking about. The whole thing is contrary to the very nature of that which we call 'building trust.'"

I remember the head of one company talking about how he kicked off his work with some big clients based on a "pinky swear."

There was an informal but very real promise made with a client about work to be done, and payment to be made, that allowed both parties to proceed immediately before all the bureaucratic paperwork was completed (those of you who work with Fortune 500 companies know all about the pain of that process). There was earned trust on both sides based on a track record of doing ethical business in a climate of mutual good will.

Frankly, a worthy reputation is a starting point for me with all of the companies I refer. If I can't trust you and feel confident that you'll add value, I can't recommend you, no matter how "good" your stuff is. *My* reputation is at stake when I make a referral.

> *"In the business of referrals, trust is the most important reason a recommendation is made and, conversely, lack of trust the single greatest reason referrals don't happen."*
> ***— John Jantsch***

For small and micro businesses especially, this is a make-or-break issue. The way to rise above the noise is to have advocates who sell for you, because they believe in you. And often, they will do so because they've had the opportunity to get to know you personally.

People remember, and refer, great networkers. Effective networking is a learned skill, and business is a long game.

But often, business networking efforts don't provide much bang for the time invested. Here's why:

1. Crop-dusting a large gathering with your business card and a few superficial introductory words may reduce your

stock of business cards, but it never increases your book of business. Referrals don't come from a momentary blip of fleeting awareness.

2. Large social gatherings might produce a lucky connection if you can actually spend some time going in-depth with another individual — but group events are typically structured so that such contacts are brief and casual. At best, you might find someone interesting that would be open to a coffee meeting in the future. The randomness factor makes these meetings questionable as far as time and effort efficiency.
3. Every networking meeting is going to feature, in some form or fashion, the question, "So, what do you do?" And, as we've seen so far in this book, a high percentage of business professionals can't answer that question in a succinct and clear fashion. Very few people have referral-ready messaging that would make their introduction to others effective and memorable, which makes for a lot of unproductive networking.
4. If you blithely assume that people (including customers!) actually know your direction, message, and bullseye client, and can articulate it to others, you will fail to equip them to be your advocates and ambassadors. When they network, they may not be spotting the right opportunities and making the right connections for you.

I happen to love business networking. Not the large-group schmoozing kind; I find those settings to be claustrophobic and my inner introvert is not in love with unstructured, noisy social settings. I'm talking about small-group discussions and one-on-one meetings over coffee. That's where real referral-producing networking can happen.

One Nashville-area group I enjoy, C-Suite Executive Breakfast, has arrived at a very effective formula for purposeful networking. During the monthly group meetings, everyone gets a brief moment to introduce themselves succinctly to the entire group (typically twenty-five to forty-five people). Then, at tables of four to six, each individual has six minutes to further explain their business and value proposition to their table group, fielding clarifying questions and telling stories. Finally, attendees gather in groups of three during the following weeks for coffee and deeper networking.

This format allows for much more focused sharing and opens the door to valuable individual relationships leading to referrals. I've gained a number of local clarity consulting clients and referrals through this type of deeper-dive networking.

I've also been heavily involved in professional/social networking through online platforms for more than a decade and developed a very active practice of meeting and connecting with great people around the world. Some of my best collaborations and business opportunities began with a tweet or a LinkedIn connection. Sometimes, those connections have remained virtual, even for years — but I can cultivate the relationships pro-actively by setting up a phone call or online video and enjoying a deeper discussion. And, in many cases, I have found ways to meet these great folks face-to-face at conferences or other travel opportunities.

We'll discuss a number of online practices in chapter 14 to help fuel your networking effectiveness and increase your visibility.

But here's the point — referral networking does not come about through wispy, barely there connections with others, either offline or online. Referral networking is the fruit of person-to-person relationships built (over time) on trust, fueled by goodwill, and informed by clarity.

Perhaps you've struggled to network effectively. In the next few chapters, we'll look at some ways to help you dramatically improve your networking game.

CHAPTER 12

Be a Questioner

Great networking isn't telling. It's asking.

It may sound counterintuitive, but those who succeed best at referral networking are those who talk the least — and ask the most.

The reason is simple: People love to talk about themselves. And they doubly love when someone takes a sincere interest in who they are and what they do. This is hard to do in a crowded room or on Twitter. It requires a dedication to getting personal with others.

As an introvert, I often used to feel inferior to my glib, gabby friends who could schmooze up a storm and light up a room. But no more inferiority complex for me. My style, which is to go deep one-on-one with individuals, gains me not just acquaintances, but also friends and advocates.

Why? Because I ask questions and listen. And then ask more questions. And keep listening. Here's the dynamic: As you listen, with focused empathy, you create connections of goodwill with others. You create intimacy, loyalty, and a sense of reciprocity — you are demonstrating kindness to others, and they want to return the favor. That's what makes people *want* to refer you.

In chapter 3 of this book, I encouraged you to master the art of storytelling. Now, we're going to look at the other side of that coin. To be a great networker, you need to become a story*asker*.

The quickest way to win someone's heart is to ask them to tell their stories.

Which stories? Well, we discussed several types of stories you can tell in chapter 3, and as it turns out, these are the very core stories you can ask others about.

1. **The evolution/origin story.** How did you get here, from wherever you started? What made you choose this course, and how did you evolve along the way? And where do you envision evolving to? One of the most interesting exercises in human networking is delving into personal and business back stories. It's always fascinating, and there are always a dozen more questions that arise along the way.
2. **The success story.** Ask about some recent (or past) business successes, and as they talk about it, drill down into the details. What was the client need that you addressed? Why did the engagement succeed? What was the customer's emotional state? You can also delve into failure stories here, especially after you first share one of your own.
3. **The how-it-felt story.** Get beyond facts, into feelings and impact. What was your relationship with your boss like? How did the downsizing affect the company atmosphere? Empathize and share common experiences. Once you're sharing at this eyeball-to-eyeball level with someone, you're well on your way to an enduring connection.

Of course, the key to becoming a good storyasker is that you're a disciplined and empathetic listener. An important component of networking is knowing how to shut up. You're not jumping in with your own stuff every 30 seconds; you're keeping the spotlight on the person across from you.

> *"Ask questions regarding feelings rather than facts. When you ask only about facts, you sound like a detective; when you inquire about feelings, you're an empathetic supporter."*
> ***— Tim Sanders***

A number of years back, I was heading to a conference in Chicago, and a lady in that city named Lisa Petrilli reached out to me before I left and asked if we could meet once I was in town. She'd done a little background research into who I was and just wanted to get to know me better. I sat in a hotel lobby with her and we had a delightful conversation — she was full of curiosity and warmth, and we stuck up a friendship that day that turned into years of professional collaboration. In fact, Lisa and I went on to host one of the better-known Twitter chats in those years, #LeadershipChat — and it all started with her proactively reaching out, asking questions, listening, and being a genuine human being.

As Dave Delaney recounts in his book *New Business Networking*: "The coffee meetings I have had have always gone longer than the 15 minutes I requested. They always end up being 30 to 60 minutes. This is because people love to talk about themselves and share their stories and wisdom."

Bob Burg, in chapter 2 of his book *Endless Referrals*, outlines ten questions that are helpful in sparking conversation, including asking about recent changes and coming trends in the marketplace, or about how the company differentiates and competes. He also includes a wonderful capstone question, which should be part of every referral networking encounter: *"How can I know if someone I'm speaking to is a good prospect for you?"* In other words, ask your conversational partner to describe their bullseye customer, so you can be a referral advocate. Once you take an interest, not only in the person, but also in their business growth, you have created a fan for life.

Of course, you'll almost always find that the other person wants to reciprocate, in which case you can describe your target marketplace and ideal customer. That's intentional referral networking, not mere socializing!

One of the benefits of intentional networking is that we can provide an outside perspective for one another. I see each networking encounter as, potentially, a mini-consulting session — I'm on the lookout for ways to provide fresh perspective or helpful advice to this person (and, often, this goes both ways). Every one of us is immersed in our professional world, enmeshed in our niche context, and because, as they say, "you can't read the label of the jar you're in," there is a great opportunity to learn from an outside perspective.

Here are several questions that can move the conversation deeper — beyond get-to-know-you inquiries, into sharing business insights:

1. How would you summarize your value proposition in 30 seconds if we met in a busy hotel lobby?

2. Where is your most profitable revenue coming from? Why? How can you increase that?
3. What's not working really well right now in your business?
4. What seems to be the most effective method for people to "get" your differentiators and make a buying decision?
5. When someone new visits your website, what do you want them to understand right away, and what action do you want them to take?

Each of these questions is digging into messaging and strategy, and surprisingly, sometimes, as a person outside of their domain or functional area you may have exactly the insight they need. Often, just by asking questions and serving as a sounding board on some of these deeper issues, you can help the person across the table to come up with their own "a-ha!" epiphany — because they just needed someone with whom to talk it through.

I was having coffee with a consultant last year who had a highly technical role in software analytics. He was a data steward — whatever that is (definitely not the most human-ready role description). By asking a bunch of questions, the imagery came into my mind: "You're that rare guy who stands between Big Data and business strategy and pulls it together for company leaders, right?" By being an outsider wanting to find human-ready language to refer him, I arrived at a word picture that underscored not just his role, but also his business value.

Plus, I got to walk away with at least half a clue about what the heck a data steward does. That has to count for something.

When you've contributed to someone's success by sharing your unique perspective, you instantly become a valuable part of their network. Being smart, generous, and open-hearted as you interact is the most effective way to build up your referral network.

This implies that you have combined being a storyasker and a provider of business perspective with a third element: You're prepared to be a human. To get to know people at more than a superficial level is to take the risk of dropping the mask and being authentic. In referral networking, your smart needs to be joined to your heart. Networking is not about collecting a series of connections and spamming them (online or offline) with sales pitches. People don't recommend pitch-makers, they recommend approachable humans who they like.

> *"There's a tidal wave coming, and it's made of people… [t]hose who win are the ones who are always prepared. [T]he winners are anticipating change and finding a ton of opportunities. You can be one of them."*
> ***— Chris Brogan and Julien Smith***

One of the best practices for successful networking is vulnerability — sharing your own stories, as appropriate, that will help the other person feel like they're not alone in the universe. Believe it or not, many people have serious questions about their direction, their decisions, and their worth. We yearn for validation and understanding from others, and if we're prepared to admit to our own weaknesses and mistakes, we powerfully open up deeper channels of communication — and attachment. Our referral advocates view us as people just like themselves, with challenges and flaws and a mixed bag of backstories. They will therefore feel comfortable recommending us to other humans because we come across, not as a threat, but as a fellow traveler.

In referral networking, your smart needs to be joined to your heart.

It is this human connection that strengthens a genuine referral network, as opposed to a mere collection of business cards and LinkedIn connections. While you don't begin your first meeting with questions about someone's recent divorce and custody battle, eventually you may, by your ongoing sincere interest, become a colleague and a confidant. Family struggles, problems with bosses, depression, painful transitions — these begin to come up naturally with people in your network as you show yourself to be trustworthy and caring. Sometimes, by asking the right question, in the right way, at the right time, you may be able to help shoulder an intolerable problem that has been festering below the surface. That's when your kindness — and perhaps a targeted referral — may help preserve someone's sanity.

Which brings us to next part of our journey into referral networking excellence: becoming a pro-active connection agent.

CHAPTER 13

Be a Connection Agent

One of the great privileges of actively networking in a business environment is making all sorts of beneficial connections between people. In fact, when I send out emails, my favorite subject line is, "You two should meet."

Why is being a connection agent so rewarding? Because the small investment of time you make sharing your contacts (in an intelligent, targeted way) can reap huge benefits for one or both parties. And the law of reciprocity is always in effect — when you've added value to others, they will usually seek to add value back to you.

The wonderful thing about being an effective connection agent is that it doesn't require an extraordinary amount of intelligence, skill, or training. It doesn't require a position of massive influence. It's simply proactive caring, and anyone can master the art.

This practice requires adopting a different perspective about networking, one centered around abundance and giving. I think of this in terms of three images:

1. **The Goldmine perspective.** Every single person in your network (including you) is a potential goldmine of knowledge, resources, and connections. In fact, the value of someone's connections may dwarf any direct value they can offer themselves.
2. **The Bigger Pie perspective.** Instead of viewing the world as a competitive field where someone has to lose if someone else wins — dividing a fixed amount of value — view connecting others as a way of creating a bigger pie. By connecting people, you multiply opportunities and help create more value for everyone.
3. **The Pinball perspective.** When you connect people, you have no idea what cool stuff might be set in motion as the timeline unfolds.

Getting to know people is a form of mining for gold. Each person has abilities, aspirations, acquaintances, and contacts; you have the privilege of bringing those riches to the surface. From there, making great connections is fueled by awareness of each other's hashtags. While a chance encounter can sometimes turn out to be valuable, of how much greater value is a deliberate "match" based on shared interests and needs?

Three of my sons have made career-shaping decisions because of intelligent network connections. By clearly describing who they were and what they were looking for, advocates could make targeted connections leading to fresh professional opportunities (two full-time jobs; one college/vocational track).

Some people I know are fabulous connection agents. They're

daily making the pie bigger for everyone. I think of my friend Thom Coats here in the Nashville area, who seems to know everybody, and who generously and diligently connects people everywhere he goes. Alana Muller's Coffee Lunch Coffee approach is a road map to making better professional connections, one which she lives out in real life. Online, I've watched Chris Brogan over the years make countless connections around the world, sharing continuously so that the pie can get bigger and bigger.

But, there's another compelling reason to be a connection agent. Your network is the new professional safety net.

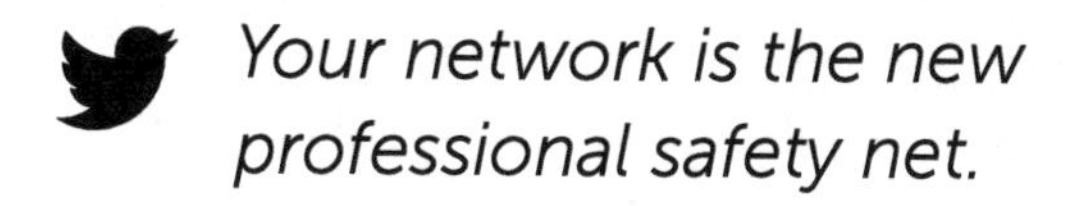

We all know that the corporate safety net is dead. Reality check: The company you work for was not built around you. It was and is built around the interests of others (shareholders, executives, customers). You are a convenience. An interchangeable tool. A means to an end.

As long as you add enough value toward the goals of others, you may have a job. When that changes, you are — how shall we say this? — an accessory that can be tossed aside. Worse yet, in today's corporation, the assessment of whether you're adding value may be up to someone who has very little idea of what you actually do.

Sounds cold, even heartless? The entire world of work is a value exchange. You're not owed a job and a stipend. And you'll add value either on your own terms or on someone else's. It's not personal; it's just business.

This means that our future is in our own hands, a topic we'll explore in-depth in Part 4. We need to build our own opportunity networks where we can much more efficiently share information, find resources, and generate new work (or job opportunities). We need to chart a future, not based on avenues opened up by some faceless corporation but fueled by organic ties to great people.

What typically happens is that people rediscover the value of a professional network during a job transition, desperately reaching out to try to secure their next position.

Sometimes that works. But what works even better is cultivating a network of great connections *before you ever need them*. This also means that you have the opportunity to add value to them and help with their needs before you ever ask for help. You've been making a bigger pie all along.

> *"The currency of real networking is not greed but generosity."*
> ***— Keith Ferrazzi***

Author and keynote speaker Dorie Clark, in her book *Stand Out*, states: "One of the best gifts you can give is to connect people who can benefit from knowing one another. If you've accrued a wide network, you probably know people who'd like to meet. Taking the time to facilitate it builds your own reputation as a giver, but it also allows amazing new things to happen — conversations, transactions, and innovations that wouldn't have been possible without the introductions you provided."

Dorie's latter point touches on a fascinating topic: networking serendipity. Like the unpredictable bounces of a pinball, you never know what is coming next as you meet people and make connections.

Back in the early days of blogging, a loose confederation of marketing bloggers began to coalesce (virtually) through blog comments, Twitter, and occasional meetups. Two of the more active connectors in the space, Drew McLellan and Christina "CK" Kerley, decided to organize Blogger Social 2008, a live networking event in NYC, which drew over seventy-five attendees from all over the world for two days of face-to-face connecting. The number of fresh connections springing from that event cannot be numbered; I still collaborate with, and refer, some of these gifted professionals to this day.

Of course, there were some unplanned consequences. One of those attendees, Arun Rajagopalan, came all the way from Oman. And he and I would play an unexpected role in an emergency two years later, when a mutual acquaintance, Leigh Fazzina, was injured during a mini-triathlon in a bicycle crash in a dimly lit park as the summer sun was setting in Connecticut. Leigh's only recourse was to use Twitter to plea for help — which Arun broadcast to his network of connections. I saw the tweets for help, as did several others, and as an ad hoc virtual team, we quickly coordinated her rescue. This was a powerful illustration of the power of connections.

Or there's this account, from blogger Lisa Petrilli:

> *A tweet I sent when on vacation in Hawaii about how I was getting rained on while dining al fresco was answered by a gentleman who was, at the same time, having breakfast on a train in Europe. I had met him very briefly months before*

> *that at a conference; we Direct Messaged each other about how Twitter brings people together from around the world and ignited a re-connection. He mentioned what he was working on — which led to me hiring him for a speaking opportunity with my client — which led to me connecting him to several members of my network — which has led to a major new account for him ... Simply put: you can never underestimate the power of a tweet — even a personal tweet — sent 'round the world.*

Networking serendipity is pervasive. The benefits of unexpected consequences remain a valuable side-effect of making connections. But as fun as these connections sometimes are, for business professionals, I mainly advocate for a deliberate approach, one that is based on clarity. If we can have conversations that impart a clear understanding of what we do and whom we serve, we equip others to make the most beneficial connections for us. And, by asking the right questions of others, we can clarify who among our contacts would be best for making a connection.

Recently I met with a gentleman in career transition. As he discussed his experience, and his future career goals, one of my past business clarity clients came to mind as a potential great match. When I brought up the name of this client, it turned out that he was already being interviewed by that very company! The clarity on both sides of the equation made the "fit" seem right for more than just one of us. (He was subsequently hired).

As a connection agent, you can occupy one of the most important pigeonholes possible in the minds of others. You become the *go-to*: The person top-of-mind when someone has a need; the one who has built up a large store of goodwill equity; and the one whom others will go to bat for when you inevitably need some help.

> *"As you connect more people together with beneficial outcomes, the level of your perceived trustworthiness goes up in the eyes of those you have connected. This allows you to build even stronger relationships with more people. It's a multiplier effect."*
> **— Chris Brogan and Julien Smith**

A connection agent is constantly thinking about targeted referrals. "Who can help this person? And how can I help put them together?" Companies can go under. Investments can go south. But being a hub, a connector of people, is one of the most secure positions you can occupy. And you can hire yourself for the role!

Connection agents tend to stand out from the crowd. Let's now take a look at how we can maximize our visibility within our networks.

CHAPTER 14

Be Visible

Winning the sales and referral game means staying top-of-mind. Even middle-of-mind will do in a pinch.

Out-of-mind, however, is a losing strategy.

Since people can easily forget who you are and what you do, you need to figure out ways to refresh their memories and spark positive feelings. That means that you have to stay visible by periodically making an appearance in the minds of your audiences.

There are many traditional ways to do this, of course: advertising, billboards, mailings, PR campaigns, and so on. These are broad reach tactics: Get to as many eyes and ears as possible and hope something sticks at the right time. It's a numbers game, and like most forms of gambling, it's hard to win.

Increasingly, there are also broad reach tactics in online platforms. The potential to reach people by broadcasting on Twitter, Facebook, Instagram, YouTube, blogs, LinkedIn, and similar platforms is irresistible, because anybody can create and publish content for these platforms. In fact, it's so irresistible that millions of people are now doing it, and the digital competition is immense. Even for those using targeted ad placements, say, via Facebook, the rest of a user's Facebook stream is generally of far more interest to them than some advertisement.

In all of these situations, you're still fighting a pitched battle with the noise. You're hoping that by getting in front of enough eyeballs, some tiny percentage will actually respond and enter your sales funnel. Over time, some percentage of that percentage will actually make a purchase. If your reach is broad enough, maybe a few qualified leads will convert at the narrow end of the funnel — but it's challenging to identify those few leads. And for small or micro companies, this approach is an exhausting and expensive exercise.

So how can you win? Let's look at three ways you can stay visible with your bullseye customers without breaking the bank: *narrowcasting*, *direct messaging*, and *delighting*.

The point of broadcasting is trying to reach the maximum number of people. It's a great strategy for Nike, because everyone needs shoes. But most companies don't need to be visible to billions, or millions, or even thousands. As we discussed in chapter 7, you'll have a far more efficient approach if you aim at your bullseye. This means painting a portrait of your most likely buyers and asking the question, "how can I reach *them*?" That's narrowcasting: targeted communications aimed at a targeted audience through the most effective platform(s).

Catherine Morgan (Point A to Point B Transitions) provides career transition coaching and business consulting for solo consultants. Her clients are transitioning from entrepreneur to corporate employee or reworking their consulting business so they actually enjoy their work and their clients. She also helps corporate employees transition to new corporate positions. This is very much a referral-driven business, but a lot of referrals happen via digital platforms now. Guess which platform Catherine uses most actively for writing posts and sharing resources?

a. Twitter
b. Instagram
c. LinkedIn

The answer, of course, is LinkedIn. That's where people in career transition tend to hang out. And that's where her content will be most sharable and relevant. Her content is focused on career topics, not leadership development or supply chain efficiency, so it is aimed at her ideal client. She, like thousands of others, is taking advantage of free (or low-cost) tools to create better visibility by narrowcasting.

Narrowcasting allows small businesses or even individuals to carve out a place of leadership in their niche. Many consultants I know have sought to establish themselves as thought leaders in their particular sweet spots. A thought leader is someone who has a particular expertise in a well-defined area of the business marketplace, joined to a consistent practice of sharing helpful information with their target audience. Mark Schaefer has become a thought leader in the marketing/social media space, while Anthony Iannarino shares constant insights in the realm of sales. Each has kept a relentless focus on his niche, and both are continually expanding their spheres of influence through blogs, books, podcasts, and speaking.

Dorie Clark says: "In thought leadership, sometimes you succeed by going big — Robert Cialdini cracking the code of influence and persuasion, or Rita McGrath explaining how business can thrive amid the end of competitive advantage. But other times, depending on your passions and goals, it's better to narrowcast … you can become the go-to authority on a particular slice … an area where your extensive knowledge, and ability to communicate it, shines."

You will often hear marketers speak about the importance of having an email list. Despite the constant predictions about the demise of email, it has remained one of the most reliable channels for reaching an audience, especially in the business realm. Building up a list of subscribers for your narrowcast email strategy is still a powerful way to remain visible to your target audience. They have opted-in to hearing from you. If you continue to entertain and inform them, you gain a regular spot in their consciousness. Regularly touching a devoted group of 100 subscribers is far better than reaching 100,000 strangers with a random message on Twitter.

I, and many other niche professionals, use blog posts and videos to reach my audiences through platforms like Facebook and LinkedIn. You can also incorporate these pieces of content into communications to your email subscribers. Focus on creating (and curating) valuable bits of content for a narrowly defined audience that has already raised their hand to hear from you. Your goal isn't to broadcast to the world. It's to narrowcast to your bullseye audience.

Your goal isn't to broadcast to the world. It's to narrowcast to your bullseye audience.

Even more precise than narrowcasting, of course, is *direct messaging*. And by this, I mean sending personalized, individual messages to another human being. In this era of blanket messaging and inbox spam, it is now remarkable to send and receive warm, personal messages. An excellent practice is to invest 15 to 20 minutes each day to send quick messages, comment on status updates, and forward relevant or interesting links to others in your network. People are so used to official, task-related communications that a personal note can make an outsized impact on the strength of the relationship. Whether a text message, an email, or (heaven forbid!) an actual written letter, these communications rise above all the noise.

Think about the impact that that last warm, unexpected message you received from someone (especially a business colleague) had on you. You deleted a thousand other messages that will never again be remembered, but when someone writes a thoughtful and personal message — it sticks. So very few people reach out with a warm touch, so those who do immediately stand out.

As I sit at my desk writing this chapter, I'm thinking back over the last couple months, trying to remember any such upbeat communication that has come my way. I'm coming up pretty empty. If that experience is typical, it means you have an open opportunity to earn a tremendous amount of visibility just by proactively reaching out and touching someone. There doesn't seem to be much competition.

I have a number of consulting clients in the pharmaceutical industry. They see a regular stream of narrowcast messages from me, via email or LinkedIn or other means. But when their company announces good news — say, a new drug approval — I like to send a personalized message with a link to the news release and a simple word of congratulations. It's amazing what the response rate is to that little unexpected touch.

How can you be more proactive direct-messaging your bullseye clients?

- Take advantage of the birthday and new job role notifications on LinkedIn and Facebook to send a quick note of congratulations; these milestones can serve as a reminder to you to give and gain an update from that individual.
- Find articles of interest about your niche market and forward them along with a quick personal note ("I thought you might find this interesting…").
- Ask their opinion about something ("What do you think of the perspective of this industry leader?").
- Ask for help with something you need or are curious about. The biggest response I get from all of my messaging, believe it or not, is a request for help. If you've been adding value to others, they want to add value back.
- Comment on posts your connections share on social media, and re-share as appropriate. This builds goodwill and a deeper connection.

Finally, you can gain visibility by delighting the people you're connected to. Guy Kawasaki wrote an entire book on this theme, titled *Enchantment*. He wrote: "When you enchant people, your goal is not to make money from them or get them to do what you want, but to fill them with great delight."

If you view business relationships mainly as professional transactions, that's what you'll get in return. You might be on a list of potential suppliers, but, like an obscure website on Google, you don't show up at the top of the results. That top-of-mind position is for those who bring their soul with them to work and who touch their audience at a deeper level.

There are many creative ways to delight those we're connected with: I'll share a few that I regularly employ:

- Tag people you know in your social media posts (Instagram, Facebook, LinkedIn) — especially when viewing a picture that includes them. In fact, take "ussies" (group selfies) when you're with your clients at events and post those (after you have secured their permission, of course).
- Send an appropriate gift that has a long shelf life. For instance, if you send some chocolates, well, those won't last long. But if you send a well-designed mug or other keepsake, you may end up with permanent desk space and a visible reminder of your generosity.
- Ask people if you can send them a book you think they'll really benefit from. How many people proactively think to send something like that? You immediately stand out as someone who adds value.

- Introduce people. Reach out and say, "I met someone yesterday that I think you really need to talk to — can I introduce the two of you?" Sometimes, if your clients are in a big company, you actually end up introducing co-workers to each other!
- Inform your contacts about upcoming events they may be interested in. You'll be shocked at how often people have no idea what's going on, even right in their neighborhood.
- Be honest with clients about what you don't do. If they are seeking a supplier and it's not in your sweet spot, you can lie and hope to get away with it. But I have heard often from clients how much they appreciate professionals who graciously bow out and even recommend others who might be a better fit. Of course, now you're also building referral goodwill with the provider you've recommended — and they may well reciprocate down the line.
- When people go through career transition — be there. Make connections. Promote them to others. Provide moral support. You'll have a friend for life.
- Finally — invite people out for coffee, or lunch, or a drink. Be proactive. In our times of hyperconnectedness, it is easy to assume that everyone's social needs are met. Assume exactly the opposite. Just the act of taking an interest in another person is memorable.

Becoming more visible involves staying in front of people with communications infused with consideration and caring. Connecting, trust, and visibility go hand-in-hand. When we consistently extend a hand to others, they gladly extend our reach and influence.

> *"Marketing used to be about advertising, and advertising is expensive. Today, marketing is about engaging with the tribe and delivering products and services with stories that spread."*
> — ***Seth Godin***

When audience members know that you're thinking about them, and when they hear from you with regularity and relevance, then you will be the one on speed dial when they have a need. While your competition is adding to the noise, you're adding value.

By consistently adding value and becoming visible, your investment will create the most powerful business development army known to humanity: long-term advocates.

And that is what we'll consider in the next chapter.

CHAPTER 15

Cultivate Advocates

I've been involved in some form of sales for over 30 years. During all that time, I've felt this constant, almost irresistible temptation to reach out as broadly as possible in the marketplace. Even when I was convinced of the value of narrowing the focus to a much smaller group, the siren song of *more, more, more* continued to bewitch me and pull away my attention. The idea was that everyone in the target marketplace who could possibly be a customer just had to hear the message somehow. Leave no potential customer behind!

A couple years back, I analyzed of all my current contacts and customers and was startled — and really, it had been staring me in the face, there's no way I should have been startled — to recognize that the vast majority of my revenue was coming from a handful of customers. Loyal customers. Advocates.

It was a "d'oh!" level epiphany.

Advocates are the people that believe in you, your cause, your product, your service. Often, but not always, they are your paying customers; sometimes, they are business colleagues or friends. They actively seek to help you succeed by buying what you have to offer and/or encouraging others to do the same.

Your advocates are the force multipliers of your business. When you ask the question, "Who loves you, baby?", these people are the answer. Above all others, they help you succeed. They want you to win.

What makes a customer advocate different from an ordinary client? Look for these traits:

1. They possess a personal, emotional attachment to you, your brand, or your company. This is generally due to an unusually positive experience you've delivered consistently over time.
2. They look for reasons to work with you. They're already sold; they just want to buy.
3. They are well-connected with others who are potential buyers.
4. They promote your offering with minimal support or prompting.
5. They like to make a difference.

These people are your unpaid sales force. For whatever reason, they have become emotionally invested in your success. Often, the only thing they lack is a clear, accurate message about your company to make their advocacy and referrals even better.

"The purpose of a business is to create a customer who creates customers."
— Shiv Singh

Another wonderful thing about customer advocates is that they tend to bring you along as they advance to other roles or other companies. I currently serve multiple companies in the pharma/biotech space who've contracted with me because my advocates had moved to new, more responsible roles within those companies. In one case, I had shown a personal and professional interest for years in a woman who did not yet have any purchasing influence. Because of that strong connection, when she became a director of training at a new company, she made internal introductions that opened up multiple business opportunities for me.

Advocates can be the difference between an organization that succeeds and one that folds — especially in the early days of a company. Of all the crucial elements that a startup needs to succeed, advocates who are already primed to become customers rank very high on the list of importance. These advocates have already found you to be valuable.

Jay Baer, in his book *Youtility*, writes, "You can break through the noise and the clutter and grab the attention of your customers by employing … an approach that is reliable, scalable, functional, and effective … stop trying to be amazing, and start being useful."

There is a class of professionals who don't generate advocates. No matter what the business card says, their unofficial title is "Jerk." It's a wonderful thing to compete with jerks, because their customers are ready to become advocates of the alternative: you.

While customers are generally your main advocates, there is another type of advocate you should be looking out for: the *influencer.*

Influencers are people who are well-known and well-established in your target marketplace. Their reputation is positive, and others look to them for advice and recommendations.

Typically, they have a following of some sort — in these days of social media, some have thousands or millions of followers on Twitter, Instagram, blogs, YouTube, and other platforms. Some of them have actually earned their influence by possessing expertise and serving as helpful connection agents in the B2B space. Celebrity influencers who are famous for being famous aren't generally going to be our target advocates.

Influencers have a platform. Great influencers share their platform with others.

Influencers have a platform. Great influencers share their platform with others.

Other influencers are less public than social media types, but no less powerful when they advocate for you or your offering. If these people have the ears of your buyer, you want them to be singing your tune. You'll want to take steps to get to know these people and demonstrate the value that you bring to the marketplace. Your investment in cultivating influencers is justified because they already possess a place of authority in the minds of your audience. Gaining access to others through their pre-existing influence is a much more efficient use of time and resources than hiring sales people and going out cold-calling. Remember, influencers have a valuable gold mine in their followings, and the best ones are eager to share and help if you know how to approach them wisely.

How can you accomplish this? I have cultivated influencers in the social media/marketing world for over 10 years, even as I serve as an influencer and connection agent in my own niche; let me outline a few influencer strategies I've learned along the way. I'll use some common dating/relationship analogies to illustrate the progression:

1. Generally speaking, there's very little ROI (Return on Investment) trying to get the attention of broad cultural influencers. Kim Kardashian is not going to retweet you, and Jimmy Kimmel is not inviting you onto his late-night show. These people hold sway over a broad, undifferentiated audience, not your niche marketplace.
2. There are less famous influencers in most marketplaces. Who are the individuals that people quote as experts and interview in industry publications? Who has a well-read blog or popular YouTube channel on your specific interest area? These people often welcome new connections because they already serve as hubs for your bullseye customers.
3. Confidently engage with these people, at trade shows, meetings, or online. Be a great questioner and find out more about their interests. Get to know them. You'll be a breath of fresh air. Subscribe to their social media posts and contribute succinct, value-adding comments.
4. (Don't ask for anything at this stage. You're not in a relationship yet.)

5. If you ask to connect with them on a social media platform, include a personalized note that expresses why you are interested, and that demonstrates that you know what they're posting about. They get dozens of anonymous, non-targeted requests from strangers every day. Yours will stand out.
6. (Don't ask for anything but the connection. You only just got their Twitter handle.)
7. Find something they've published — a magazine article, a picture, a blog post — and post a link to it on your social media timeline with credit and an appreciative comment. Be sure to tag them in your post so that they see your engagement.
8. (Don't ask for anything in return. You've just complimented their outfit.)
9. At some point, send a private message of some sort and just let them know you're reading/watching/learning. The nice ones are likely to reply.
10. (Don't ask for anything yet. You're just getting to know one another.)
11. Lather, rinse, repeat. Your potential advocates will begin to recognize you (through your engagement level) and hopefully will start to exchange messages with you. You'll discover that they are human beings who enjoy other human beings that treat them as human beings. Now you're in a relationship.
12. Did they write a book? Read it, and write an intelligent review on Amazon.

13. Now, perhaps, forward something small you've created (say, a blog post or a 90-second video) and ask, "what do you think?" Don't ask for exposure; just try to deepen the level of interaction.
14. Find ways to share information: Meet at a conference, or get together for coffee. Now you're on your way to creating an advocate — because you didn't try to immediately exploit them for their influence (they see it all the time and hate it. Don't be that one-night-stand guy/gal!).

Does this sound like a lot of effort? It is an investment, because you're building an important, long-term relationship, not looking for a retweet fling. Transactions can be momentary and impersonal. Advocacy is earned over time.

Some heavy-hitter influencers are super-connectors — they have a big following and seem to know everybody. At first, I was a little bit hesitant to approach super-connectors, because — well, I was suffering from some imposter syndrome and an inward sense of intimidation. Then I discovered that the ones who really mattered actually liked connecting and sharing and that I could even, at times, add value to them with knowledge and introductions of my own. The intimidation generally disappeared at the first face-to-face interaction.

Authors are influencers. And they love to hear from their readers. Reviews, comments, recommendations — these are some of the quickest ways to their hearts. One very effective approach: Take a selfie of you reading their book (with a few Post-It Notes or highlighted passages) and tag them on social media. What's better than an appreciative reader?

Finally, there's another group of potential advocates you can cultivate, and that is your network of *local people*. It is far easier to get together with people near your geographical area, and there is already a base of shared life and acquaintances. You can build trust more rapidly when you can get together for coffee and face-to-face interaction, and local people are sometimes more open than distant contacts to making introductions and opening new doors. Sometimes, your local influencers hold the key to reaching other influencers in your sphere.

Besides, your neighborhood coffee shop really, really wants you to practice local networking.

For those that are non-local but still open to chat, videoconferencing is the way to go. You can even share a virtual cup of coffee or glass of wine as you talk. Digital marketing consultant Tom Martin and I sometimes schedule late afternoon video chats over bourbon.

One of the best ways to cultivate advocates is to be an advocate. Promote other people's work on your social feed. Put a spotlight on those less-known in your industry. Make introductions and recommendations of people without any quid pro quo anticipation of return. Organize meetups. Help others with career transitions. What's in it for you? You might not see something tangible in the short term, but in the long term, you're building an army of people who will always be on your side. These people will open doors, promote you, and make referrals. You're crafting your safety net and opportunity network.

Referral networking is, in essence, a posture of giving in action.

Few excel at it because it takes long-term vision, an open heart, and a pro-active mindset. You don't need exceptional talent to excel at this practice. You just need to act. And you have all the tools at hand to assemble and activate your referral network.

Referral networking is, in essence, a posture of giving in action.

By investing in your network, you're investing in your future. And if clarity drives us to anything, it's to thinking intelligently about the future.

For additional resources, including helpful forms and videos, please visit **www.claritywins.online**.

Enjoying *Clarity Wins* so far? Head on over to **www.claritywins.net**, where we make it easy for you to share highlights on your favorite social channels!

PART 4

Designing your Future

INTRODUCTION

Designing a Future of Growing Opportunities

Earlier in this book, we referenced Apple's ad campaign, "Think Different."

Gaining clarity is a call to do just that — put aside your old, limiting beliefs and think about your business and your future opportunities in a different way.

You don't have to be confined to the way things were, or even the way things are. Whether you're growing a business or making a career transition, you can look at the future as something you get to design — or at least, your little slice of it.

You can set aside some limiting mindsets once you're fueled by clarity. The biggest stumbling block is the idea that the world has given you a fixed menu, and you have to conform to the labels, norms, business entities, and procedures that have been established for you. That's hogwash. You don't have to be an interchangeable part in someone else's machine.

The future — *your* future — is up to you to design.

It is liberating to realize that every single thing that surrounds us today was designed by other people for needs that they perceived at the time. Some of those structures and methods and objects will carry into the future, but many of them are already well on their way to obsolescence. We don't have to be limited by what we've come to think of as normal or inevitable. New challenges, new technologies, new jobs — that's the new normal.

Artificial intelligence is about to make its way into everything around us. 3D printing: Who would have guessed that manufacturing would be decoupled from factories? Entire houses are now being printed on-site.

In agrarian days, most work took place at home. Later, everyone "went" to work. Now, work is anywhere and everywhere for huge swaths of the population. Technology-driven change is disrupting industry ecosystems and creating entirely new roles and approaches at an increasing rate.

You have a future to design. You can adjust your mindset to help turn your clarity into years of growth and opportunity. When it comes to the role you will play and the job you will do, you needn't think small. There's no limit on the number of potential avenues you can pursue. You can focus your efforts, evolve your direction, and win.

As you move forward into a world of abundance, let's first consider the opportunity you have to not only survive or contribute, but to actually dominate.

CHAPTER 16

Dominating Niches

The most audacious leaders in business may actually proclaim that their overarching goal is *world domination*! Maybe you've aspired to that as well, at least in jest. Fame and glamour will be yours. Your name will be in the headlines. Champagne wishes and caviar dreams are just around the corner!

Then you realize, a few years later, that your chances of reaching that lifestyle are located somewhere between slim and none. That glamorous horizon actually looks a lot more like mortgage payments and daily survival. So much for world domination.

Only a few get to pull that off. Amazon, Apple, Alphabet — these West Coast A-list tech companies are doing some serious dominating and doing it on a global scale. So, what does that leave for the rest of us?

Niche domination.

We've already covered what it means to define your niche. That's the first half the battle. Now you want to consider ways to dominate it. In a well-focused niche, even a company consisting of one person can become the dominant player. And there's plenty of money in any niche where you are scratching a genuine business itch.

> *There's plenty of money in any niche where you are scratching a genuine business itch.*

What is niche domination? It's creating, or moving into, a market space narrow enough that you can become the dominant player and expansive (or expandable) enough that you can make great revenue as you grow it.

Some people are content to be little fish in a huge pond, but you have higher aspirations. By focusing on a tightly defined niche, you and your business can become a major player. Perhaps *the* major player.

Susan Friedman had the right idea in her book titled, *Riches in Niches*. You don't need the billions of dollars (and millions of customers) that Amazon is handling every day. You just need an income that grows by solving the problems and meeting the needs of a few key customers.

Serial entrepreneur Aaron Walker puts it this way in his book, *View From The Top*: "Whatever industry you're in, you've got to narrow in, focus, and look for your exact person, your avatar. Focus allows you to define and find what your strengths are; niching down is so important because, for some reason, we always want to be all things to all people, and that is just not possible."

For a long time, there wasn't really a marketing system for small businesses. Then, to try to fill a gap, John Jantsch created one, called Duct Tape Marketing, which has grown into a worldwide marketing/consulting business. John recognized an unmet need (for himself and others): It was very difficult to buy marketing services as a small business. So, he carved out a niche, created a solution, and promoted it into a powerhouse; but it all started with creatively contemplating a problem that no one else was addressing.

As we mentioned in chapter 11, Marcus Sheridan's local swimming pool company in Virginia was in deep trouble once the 2008 economic collapse occurred. How could he survive, let alone thrive, in such a depressed marketplace? It turns out that there was a dearth of information online about swimming pools. By becoming a dominant voice using content marketing, he turned his company around and created the No. 1 ranked website in his industry.

Sheridan's story of niche domination even evolved into a new business opportunity. As his story of success spread, Marcus was then able to launch a fresh career as a speaker and writer on the subject of effective content marketing.

In the Nashville area, one family came up with a recipe for over-the-top donuts. One of their confections, a cross between a donut and a croissant, stands tall with 100 layers of goodness; the process of making one spans days, not minutes. Are there a lot of donut shops around, locally and nationally? Sure. But Five Daughters Bakery came up with a new twist on delivering decadence, and its long lines of customers spend enough money on these confections that the franchise has expanded to multiple locations. Pastry is not a new thing. Exotic pastry for the masses is relatively new, however, and creative first-movers can create fresh niche markets.

The food and beverage marketplace, in fact, is exploding with niches. Artisan foods, organic ingredients, local breweries and distilleries, farm-to-table suppliers, food trucks, vegan and gluten-free offerings — the sub-niches abound. For years, Boston Beer Company (maker of Samuel Adams) was the upstart brewer dominating the craft beer space; now, hundreds of others are establishing specialized or localized footprints in order to dominate sub-markets. New Belgium, Dogfish Head, Harpoon, Brooklyn, Allagash, Rogue, and dozens of others are creating followings among their target audiences.

I love bacon. Among the underground of bacon aficionados, there is a name that you'll hear whispered with near-reverence. Because there's bacon … and then there's Benton's Bacon. Benton's has a great back story and puts out a product that thrills the senses. "I (Allen Benson) was trying to sell quality up against other people who were quick-curing their hams in 80 days," he writes. "I told my dad that I would need to switch to a shorter cure if I was going to survive. My dad said, 'Son, if you play the other man's game, you always lose.' So, I decided to make the best I could, and quality would eventually win out."

I assure you, Allen's dad was right. Benton's wins.

Let's say that you're a real estate agent. Now there's a crowded market space! Everyone knows one or two (or twelve) real estate agents, half of which may be relatives. But I recently met one who had developed a particular subspecialty — the needs of corporate executives relocating into and out of a specific geographical area.

Those customers put a premium on speed, coordination of multiple transactions, and full-service, remove-the-friction logistics. While this type of situation is a small subset of all real estate transactions, it is a lucrative one, with plenty of repeat opportunities; the target clients come from a select few of the larger companies in the area. This opened the door to specialized niche expertise by cultivating those companies and providing a suite of targeted services focused on the relocation market.

I'm not an online gamer, but my kids are. They talk about gamers who are absolutely dominating their niche with YouTube channels on how to play and win specific games. In a one-year span during 2016 to 2017, Minecraft player Daniel Middleton had over 11 billion views on YouTube and made $16.5 million.

Ryan ToysReview now has 10 million subscribers. The channel made $11 million in revenue last year. Ryan is a seven-year-old.

How many people would have foreseen such a niche business model taking off like this, even five years ago? I wish I had.

Assuming that you're not jumping into a YouTube channel business model, how can you move from niche targeter to niche dominator? Pursue these strategies as you expand your footprint:

1. Find a niche or even a sub-niche that isn't saturated. Sometimes moving from commodity provider to dominant player is all about identifying an even smaller niche where you can specialize. Home improvement services is not a niche. Building custom man-cave bars using reclaimed wood in a local, wealthy market — that's a niche with domination potential.

2. Catch a wave early. Joel Comm made a fortune with farts. How? Early on, he recognized how big the iPhone app marketplace would become, and he launched a whimsical program called iFart that quickly became a best seller. He spotted the trends and jumped in (see more on trend currents in chapter 17).
3. Create a fresh angle to your offering that others can't or won't match. It can be as simple as a free return policy (Nordstrom used this approach effectively for years to help build a rabid customer base) or Amazon Prime Wardrobe's recent move to allow customers to try clothing and return what they don't want to keep. For a micro business, it can be as simple as a hand-written note card included with the product, or a $10 gift card of appreciation, or a bonus 1-hour consultation (live or virtually) with an expert. Cultivating an add-value approach will make you remarkable, memorable, referral-ready, and eventually dominant.
4. Provide fanatical customer service. So many companies do the bare minimum and don't even try to be outstanding in creating a great customer experience. To attain a dominant position, be the market leader in happy customers. Southwest Airlines is famous for its fun, personal approach to interacting with customers, and its following has been loyal for decades. As I've told my adult kids many times, all you have to do to rise above 90% of the crowd is be nice, responsible, respectful, and hard-working. That's true of businesses, too.

5. If you're worth more, charge more. One of the most common practices I've come across in startups and micro businesses is under-charging for services. You generally want to occupy the position of a top-tier provider, and you want to attract customers who don't mind paying a premium for excellence. Skilled photographer Jeremy Cowart is going to produce exceptional images, and his price point, therefore, won't be in the average range. He's not competing with high school kids slinging iPhones. Dominant players aren't racing to the bottom in an unwinnable price war. That's the commodity zone, where only the biggest companies can dominate.
6. For top executives, entrepreneurs, and consultants: Plant your flag as the go-to thought leader for your niche. If there isn't already a go-to, strive to become one, or at least act out the part as you make it a reality through skillful content marketing. Yes, that takes a bit of moxie, but as it turns out, you don't have to be the smartest or the biggest to start dominating. You mainly have to be bold and consistently visible (see chapter 14). By regularly adding helpful value to those inside, and adjacent to, your niche, you start to occupy that pigeonhole in their minds as the authority, the key resource. Social tools like LinkedIn and YouTube make it possible for anyone to become a public figure that gains attention and respect by sharing solid content.
7. Seek to become the "mayor" of your niche. The mayor is the one who gets to know a lot of people and makes

connections behind the scenes. Serving as a niche connection agent creates immense goodwill over time and also positions you as the one who seems to know everyone. Several years ago, someone in my pharma training market space dubbed me "The Mayor of LTEN" (Life Sciences Trainers & Educators Network), and the identity stuck. There may be hundreds or thousands of people in your niche, but there's only one mayor! It's advice as old as time, but it's still true: Show up, shake hands, grab a drink, kiss babies, make introductions. You don't have to be the SEO King of Google to be the human mayor of your market space.

8. Stay the course. Very few businesses can build a dominant position without long-term consistency. If you know there's gold in that niche, set yourself on a long-term path of investing time and effort into mining it.

It's very easy to think that you cannot occupy a prominent place in your market, but with a few changes in perspective, and practices such as those suggested above, you create a pathway to success. Dominating your niche begins with asking and answering the question, "Why not me/us?"

Gaining clarity will also propel you to ask other "why not?" questions. Clear vision leads to opportunistic visualization. In the next chapter, we'll see that many business opportunities lie on the other side of that simple inquiry.

CHAPTER 17

Visualizing Opportunities

Opportunity is perpetual and growing.

It's easy to think that people have already come up with all the good ideas. Not even close. In fact, good ideas that can turn into business opportunities are essentially infinite.

Technology keeps progressing (exponentially). Barriers to connection and commerce keep shrinking. Information keeps expanding. Population keeps growing (and aging).

This means that there always more edges, more niches, more pain points, more needs, and more gaps and disconnects. The only limit is our ability to recognize the endlessly evolving pool of needs and put together some way to match a solution to a pain point (or desire).

A popular term for this approach was coined by W. Chan Kim and Renée Mauborgne in the bestselling book *Blue Ocean Strategy*. The subtitle of the book says it all: "How to create uncontested market space and make the competition irrelevant." Doesn't that sound wonderful — irrelevant competition? All you'll have to do is stand out from the noise.

The authors distinguish between established market spaces (red oceans), and new ones (blue oceans). "In the red oceans, industry boundaries are defined and accepted, and the competitive rules of the game are known. Here, companies try to outperform their rivals to grab a greater share of existing demand … products become commodities, and cutthroat competition turns the red ocean bloody."

Blue oceans, on the other hand, are untapped market spaces, where you can create new demand and set new boundaries. Entrepreneurs can sometimes visualize blue lagoons along the edges of red oceans and carve out fresh niches to dominate.

That's why we can afford to adopt a mindset of constant, creative opportunism. The marketplace is not fixed, nor is it rigged. As you gain clarity about who you are and what you are capable of, then the world around you reveals itself to be a wide-open field just waiting for new ideas.

The best way to visualize new opportunities is to keep a finger on the pulse of what I call *trend currents. Current trends* are visible shifts, often extending what's already happening, but *trend currents* are big-picture, unstoppable, inexorable forces that are shaping the world we live in. A current trend would be the incremental move toward electric cars. Trend currents, however, are causing a complete re-thinking of how we use cars for transportation. Will we own cars or just buy access to them when we need them? Will we, or AI (artificial intelligence), be the drivers in the future? Will other forms of transportation (such as the futuristic Hyperloop) begin to make cars obsolete?

Trend currents are big-picture, unstoppable, inexorable forces that are shaping the world we live in.

Uber did not create the dominant ride-sharing service by cobbling together another taxi company. The existing models, such as taxis, limousines, buses, and rental cars, were well-established, with big players already entrenched (and fighting each other in the red ocean). Uber came about because a visionary leader saw the convergence of trend currents (ubiquitous mobile devices, GPS, gig economy) and unmet needs (low-cost, quick, convenient transport) and devised a new platform that has upended the marketplace. Thus was established a new niche, a fresh opportunity to create and dominate.

Uber is huge, but these same converged forces also create small, lucrative niches. In recent years, Jessica (Ostroff) Tyson launched Don't Panic Management, offering virtual assistant services. Instead of needing a full-time (or local) assistant, a whole market space has developed around fractional, virtual services to support businesses and executives with administrative and other tasks. This type of business became possible because of the conjunction of web technology (work from anywhere), collaborative software (work with others), and a move toward part-time, on-demand services.

These trend currents have led to the creation of a whole new areas of value-adding efficiency in the realm of contracted, fractional expertise and service. New niche businesses like Jessica's pop up daily. Converging trend currents are fertile seedbeds of opportunity. It's a great time to be an entrepreneur!

The cracking of the human genetic code has led to major breakthroughs in the area of personalized medicine, a massive trend current that will impact healthcare for decades to come. On the smaller scale, cheap technology now allows companies to custom-create a personalized pair of jeans for any customer.

In computing, security and privacy challenges are going to be a major frontier for development, along with tools for sifting, filtering, and pattern-matching massive pools of data. There is no stopping the tsunami of information pouring from people and objects. In all likelihood, the next set of fortunes will be made, not in generating more information, but in filtering and combining all that data into useful packages that enable better decisions.

We need to see, not just where the market has come from historically, but where it is going over the next 5 to 10 years. Right now would not be a good time to invest in a company designing word processing software or manufacturing fax machines. Those days have come and gone. But, AI? That's already shaping virtually every aspect of the future. Voice-activated devices like Alexa, Google Home, and Siri are only the beginning. Billions of dollars are flowing there.

Beside the freelance workforce movement mentioned above, and the explosion of AI, here is a sampling of other trend currents shaping our society that are providing ongoing fresh opportunities for creative business approaches:

1. The aging population (a challenge in multiple countries around the world as lifespans grow longer and fewer children are born). This has large ramifications in the realms of healthcare and lifestyle.
2. Disintermediation through technology (example: what Amazon has done to book publishers, printers, and distributors). Automation is a subset of this: the replacement of inefficient humans with machines.
3. The steady replacement of printed materials by video (fueled by the availability of anytime/anywhere bandwidth and mobile devices).
4. Expanding challenges in security and privacy. Blockchain and similar technologies are attempting to provide solutions to this problem.
5. Support for local/personalized/natural/craft businesses (in opposition to imported/industrial/artificial/mass products provided by mega-corporations).

We can *know* that these inexorable movements will disrupt current markets and create fresh opportunities. Picture yourself standing at a fast-flowing river, ready to launch your canoe. Do you think you'll get somewhere faster heading downstream with the current, or do you want to go upstream against the flow?

Years ago, in the earliest days of the public world wide web, I saw the future. I intuitively understood that this was going to be big. But what I didn't grasp was the virtual "land grab" of claiming domains (URLs) for a few bucks, which could then be resold for thousands or even millions of dollars.

I'd be sitting on a beach somewhere if I'd just grabbed www.travel.com, or www.money.com, or a thousand other domain names that inevitably grew in value exponentially. Other, more visionary people figured out the impending value of virtual real estate in the Internet world that was coming fast. You can find them on beaches while I'm still writing books!

Amazon, combined with Whole Foods and home delivery services, is demonstrating what the future of instant gratification looks like. The merger of online convenience, brick-and-mortar presence, and speed of delivery is creating a whole new trend current in retail.

The world of work has changed dramatically in the last couple decades. Previously, the vast majority of people worked for *other-based* businesses. Someone else's company. Someone else's product or service. Someone else's customers. Someone else's structure of titles, compensation, work patterns, and direction. And, frequently, there were mismatches. People experienced the frustration of not fitting into a certain company or role.

> *"Don't accept the lie that work has to be miserable and dreams are for other people. They are for everyone."*
> ***— Jon Acuff***

Having a clarity-fueled approach gives you the option of considering a me-based business. An exercise I've used with people looking for new professional opportunities is called "Role Your Own": What exactly would the ideal business (or job role) look like if you could build it around your own unique strengths and aspirations? Once you've mapped that out, it's time to approach the marketplace with that clarity-fueled filter in place, instead of grasping at pre-existing business roles that might not be a good match.

My friend Kevin Kruse puts it this way: "If you aren't busy working on your own goals, you'll be working to achieve somebody else's goals."

As you consider new business opportunities, you, like a surfer, want to catch waves that are already moving toward the shore — including the increasingly common option of defining your own work. Don't just think about what's always worked in the past. The old, fixed categories are fading away. Think about how Peloton has tapped into the combination of ubiquitous video streaming, healthy lifestyle, and virtual community to bring a whole new approach to home workouts.

You're not even limited to traditional job or business roles. Carol Roth, in her book The Entrepreneur Equation distinguishes between what she has coined as Jobbies (a hobby disguised as a job or business); Job-Businesses (a business whose value is primarily dependent upon one or a handful of people); and Bona-Fide Businesses (an entity that has equity value and is not dependent on any one individual). Each of these approaches has merits, and each business model can evolve in one direction or another as conditions change.

There are ten thousand opportunities on the horizon. Then ten thousand more next week. The pie keeps growing and, in a rapidly evolving marketplace, white spaces and blue oceans will continue to surround us.

You're launching your skills and your offerings into a universe of abundance, and as the market changes, you get to sharpen your focus and evolve with it. Remember, clarity is not a one-time process. It's ongoing.

CHAPTER 18

Gaining and Maintaining Focus

It was 1962, and the United States was in the middle of the space race with the Soviet Union. It was time to rally the country's leaders and citizens around a big goal — an expensive, risky endeavor called the Apollo program.

President John F. Kennedy stood up at Rice Stadium in Houston, Texas, and, on September 12, uttered these memorable words:

> *We choose to go to the Moon in this decade and do the other things, not because they are easy, but because they are hard; because that goal will serve to organize and measure the best of our energies and skills, because that challenge is one that we are willing to accept, one we are unwilling to postpone, and one we intend to win.*

Part of what made this challenge so effective is that it was specific — there was a time (this decade), a place (the Moon), and a goal (win the race). There was clear focus, clear purpose, and a bullseye target.

Imagine, however, if JFK had tried to engender support with a bunch of mushy generalities:

We hope to send a rocket-boosted exploration solution into space with the idea that, among the billions of stars in our Milky Way galaxy, and the billions of galaxies beyond, we might land some of our stuff out there in the vast reaches of the universe sometime before we're extinct as a species.

Not quite so inspiring, right? Let's just launch that thing and see where it goes!

"Where focus goes, energy flows."
— Tony Robbins

No great deed was ever accomplished without focus: a defined direction and purpose. We say "yes!" to very specific things, which implies that we are actively saying "no!" to the alternatives. Olympic athletes win by focusing on one sport, not several.

Gaining business clarity is about finding focus: looking at what we have, what we do, and what is around us, and choosing the most productive and profitable path forward.

No great deed was ever accomplished without focus — a defined direction and purpose. Olympic athletes win by focusing on one sport, not several.

When I was in grade school, and my eyesight was changing (for the worse) each year, I remember the moment in the fall when

I'd first put on a new pair of glasses with a fresh prescription. Everything was suddenly back in focus! I had drifted into a state of blur, unconsciously compensating for the myopia and not realizing that I wasn't seeing the world clearly at all.

Every business periodically needs a new prescription in order to see the world in focus.

Typically, I've seen individuals and business reach clarity in two stages — the epiphany stage and the evolutionary stage.

In the epiphany stage, there is a coming together of various (previously blurry) strands into a burst of enlightenment — what was foggy and indefinite suddenly begins to make sense in a whole new way. Just a week before writing this chapter, I had one of those moments in an all-day business coaching session about the future of my clarity practice. There were loose ends all around, clients and ideas and offerings that I just couldn't quite put together, until an outside coach (who knows me and my work) helped brainstorm it with me and turn it all into a much clearer map.

Often, those who are feeling lost in the fog and needing a fresh epiphany fall into one of these categories:

1. Business startups with great ideas and some raw talent, but without a clear offering for a well-defined niche market space.
2. Solo consultants who are having trouble differentiating themselves from all the other potential providers.
3. Established businesses that have taken on too many different types of projects or services and now no longer have a differentiated offering or message.

4. Individuals in career transition, typically between ages 35 and 65, with a long enough track record to analyze their strengths and determine their true sweet spot.

You can think of this stage as starting with a box of Legos: We dump them all out on the table, sort by shape and function, then put it all together into something useful. Epiphanies about business direction generally need someone from the outside — an objective third party — to help us see beyond our blind spots and gain fresh focus. It's a bit like a therapy session, helping put the pieces together and seeing the big picture. We all need this kind of wise input; that's the reason for business coaches and consultants.

Setting the compass after a fresh epiphany of clarity is like experiencing that feeling of walking out of the optometrist's office with new glasses. The area of your pigeonhole becomes clearer, and your message is distilled. At this point, I give people the advice I gave myself when I launched my own company — I can map out my direction to about the 85% level, and now the marketplace is going to have to help figure out the other 15%.

In other words, to succeed in business, you not only set the destination in your GPS, but as you seek to get from A (where you are right now) to B (that newly defined direction), you recognize there will be some adjustments and detours along the way.

That's the evolutionary stage of ongoing clarity. As we've discussed before, nothing will remain static in your marketplace, and you need to be prepared to edit, tweak, and pivot as conditions change or as fresh client needs arise.

Nothing will remain static in your marketplace, and you need to be prepared to edit, tweak, and pivot as conditions change or as fresh client needs arise.

Pamela Wilson began her career as a graphic designer — and she is still a good one. She started her own marketing firm and design studio in 1992. But then she moved her business online and launched Big Brand System in 2010, where she became more immersed in the world of online marketing. There, she helps people build online businesses with her professional coaching and community for entrepreneurs. As her audience grows, she taps into her own sweet spots and adapts her offerings.

Anthony Iannarino began his sales career with the family staffing business in 1989. As he grew that business, others began asking him for help and advice on selling. He began actively using social media to share his insights in 2008 and made a commitment to blog daily about sales in 2010 with the goal (achieved!) of becoming a keynote speaker by year-end. Now a published author and international thought leader on sales, Anthony leads a multi-million-dollar business providing training and consulting on sales, sales leadership, and organizational transformation. The market sought more and deeper expertise, and he evolved to meet those needs.

I've seen this type of evolution frequently. The core DNA and strengths remain intact, but you may need to shift the audience and refine the message over time.

Think of your pigeonhole as your 85% zone. You've carefully defined what you're offering, and to whom, and you keep that message simple for the sake of generating referral-ready messaging. But, you may still keep 15% of what you do in your back pocket — side-hustle work, related offerings, new ideas — and as you move forward in your marketplace, you might see your sweet spot expand or shift. Unforeseen opportunities may present themselves. If you've found a new gold mine of bullseye customers, then you may have the delightful opportunity to clarify your message and re-pigeonhole yourself, not because you made a mistake before, but because you're evolving and winning with fresh clarity.

Brian Moran had 22 years of experience in small-business development and strategy when he launched his third company, Brian Moran & Associates, a consultancy to help business owners run better companies. He had two audiences as he began: entrepreneurs and small-business owners who were stuck and in need of strategic help; and enterprise-level clients seeking to provide services for SMBs. Over time, providing deeper strategic expertise (strategy, communications, execution) to the large corporations evolved into the most profitable line of work. To continue serving the smaller companies, Brian relaunched his existing website, Small Business Edge, into a membership community of support and resources.

A word of caution, however: Some businesses, and especially some entrepreneurs, can't settle on one thing when it comes to business focus. Their direction and message are changing constantly. In the fast-paced online and technology space, this is a real danger. If you yourself are a moving target, no-one will know how to refer you, even if they admire your energy and initiative. It may be that every high-energy entrepreneur needs to identify a business coach that will help them distinguish between real opportunity and creative itchiness.

What keeps us on track is embracing an overarching vision for our lives and businesses. We want to program the GPS so that the decisions we're making today help us move toward, not away from, our big-picture destination. Clarity at the level of overarching direction will cascade down to clarity in a host of smaller choices and keep us on track even as we react to and evolve with a dynamic marketplace.

> *"That's been one of my mantras — focus and simplicity. Simple can be harder than complex. You have to work hard to get your thinking clean to make it simple. But it's worth it in the end because once you get there, you can move mountains."*
> ***— Steve Jobs***

Winning in business is hard work, even in the best of circumstances. But we don't want to make it harder for ourselves by having an unfocused strategy and a muddled message. By fueling all that we do and say with clarity, we stand the best possible chance of slaying the Goliaths that oppose us and spreading our message through those who want to help us win.

You read this book because you want to win. I wrote this book because I want you to be a winner. Drop me a line and let me know how I can help you as we pursue niche domination together!

Steve Woodruff

steve@clarityfuel.com

Thank you so much for reading *Clarity Wins*! Will you now do me a huge favor? Please take a minute and share your review of the book on Amazon. That's how you can help me be heard and be referred!

ENDNOTES

Part 1 Introduction: Knowing your Enemy

Only half of all new establishments are still operating after 5 years: "Do nine out of 10 news businesses fail, as Rand Paul claims?" by Glenn Kessler, from Washington Post, January 27, 2014. See http://bit.ly/CWins_1

Chapter 1: Facing the Enemy

Malcolm Gladwell, *David and Goliath: Underdogs, Misfits, and the Art of Battling Giants*, Back Bay Books; Reprint edition (April 7, 2015), p. 14-15.

Thomas H. Davenport and John C. Beck, *The Attention Economy: Understanding the New Currency of Business*, Harvard Business Review Press; Revised edition, (September 2002), p. 11.

the average American spent 11 hours per day consuming: "Americans are now spending 11 hours each day consuming media" by Ashley Rodriguez, from Quartz, July 30, 2018. See http://bit.ly/CWins_2

the average American checks their smartphone eighty times per day: "Americans check their smartphones 80 times a day: study" from Today.com, November 11, 2017. See http://bit.ly/CWins_3

vary from 3,000 to 20,000 exposures per day: "New research sheds light on daily ad exposures" by Sheree Johnson, from SJ Insights, September 29, 2014. See http://bit.ly/CWins_4

the average office worker gets only 11 minutes: "The cost of interrupted work: more speed and stress" by Gloria Mark, University of California Irvine, and Daniela Gudith/Ulrich Klocke, Humboldt University. See http://bit.ly/CWins_5

"Content Shock": "Content Shock: why content marketing is not a sustainable strategy" by Mark Schaefer, from Businesses Grow blog. See http://bit.ly/CWins_6

The RAS is responsible for awareness: "Functions of Reticular Activating System (RAS)" from psychologydiscussion.net. See http://bit.ly/CWins_7

The RAS is responsible for...focus and attention prioritization: "Structure and functions of the Reticular Activating System (RAS)" from bodytomy.com, December 21, 2017. See http://bit.ly/CWins_8

Chapter 2: Breaking through the Barriers

Apple 1984 Super Bowl commercial introducing Macintosh computer, from YouTube. See http://bit.ly/CWins_9

Nate Woodruff, WhiskyWithAView, Instagram. See http://bit.ly/CWins_10

Angela Maiers, angelamaiers.com. See http://bit.ly/CWins_11

Donald Miller, *Building a StoryBrand: Clarify Your Message So Customers Will Listen*, HarperCollins Leadership; (October 10, 2017), p. 4.

Microsoft released a study: "Microsoft attention spans research report" from Microsoft Canada on Scribd, Spring 2015. See http://bit.ly/CWins_12

David Rock, *Your Brain at Work: Strategies for Overcoming Distraction, Regaining Focus, and Working Smarter All Day Long*, HarperBusiness; 1 edition (October 6, 2009), p. 25.

Mary Matalin, James Carville, Peter Knobler: *All's Fair: Love, War and Running for President*, Simon and Schuster; (1995), p. 175.

"55% or visitors to media sites": "What you think you know about the web is wrong" by Tony Haile, from Time, March 9, 2014. See http://bit.ly/CWins_13

Milo O. Frank, *How to Get Your Point Across in 30 Seconds or Less*, Gallery Books; (Reissue edition April 15, 1990), p. 14.

Chapter 3: Telling your Stories

Jonathan Gottschall, *The Storytelling Animal: How Stories Make Us Human*, Mariner Books; 1 edition (April 23, 2013), p. xiv.

activate multiple areas of the brain: "Your brain on stories" by Susan Weinshenck, Ph.D., from Psychology Today, November 4, 2014. See http://bit.ly/CWins_14

Robert McKee: *Story: Substance, Structure, Style, and the Principles of Screenwriting*, (HarperCollins 1997). See also: mckeestory.com, http://bit.ly/CWins_15

WhistlePig Distillery, whistlepigwhiskey.com.

Jimmy Neil Smith, International Storytelling Center. See http://bit.ly/CWins_16

Thomas Clifford, nomorejagon.com. See http://bit.ly/CWins_17

Donald Miller, storybrand.com. See http://bit.ly/CWins_18

Seth Godin, *All Marketers Are Liars*, (Portfolio, 2009 Edition), p. 105.

Susan Cain, The Power of Introverts (Ted Talk video). See http://bit.ly/CWins_19

Bernadette Jiwa, *Story Driven: You don't need to compete when you know who you are*, Perceptive Press; 1 edition (February 27, 2018), p. 57.

customers are willing to tell their stories about you: "A customer service story with a Gaping Void in it" by Steve Woodruff, from stevewoodruff.com blog, January 6, 2014. See http://bit.ly/CWins_20

Chapter 4: Speaking Human

Blue Spoon Consulting, bluespoonconsulting.com. See http://bit.ly/CWins_21

"The Curse of Knowledge": *"The Sense of Style: The Thinking Person's Guide to Writing in the 21st Century"* by Steven Pinker (Viking 2014) p. 57. See http://bit.ly/CWins_22

Hubspot: hubspot.com. http://bit.ly/CWins_23

Tate Parker, tateparker.com. See http://bit.ly/CWins_24

Quantum Learning, quantumlearninginc.com.
See http://bit.ly/CWins_25

Ann Handley and C.C. Chapman, *Content Rules: How to Create Killer Blogs, Podcasts, Videos, Ebooks, Webinars (and More) That Engage Customers and Ignite Your Business*, Wiley; Revised and Updated edition (May 22, 2012), p. 31.

Part 2 Introduction: Choosing your niche

Richard Branson, Twitter, September 3, 2012. See http://bit.ly/CWins_26

Chapter 5: The Five Elements of Clarity

Brains on Fire, brainsonfire.com. See http://bit.ly/CWins_27

Simon Sinek, TEDxPuget Sound, September 28, 2009. See http://bit.ly/CWins_28

Chapter 6: Getting in your Zone

Steve Jobs, quoted in Fortune Magazine, March 7, 2008. See http://bit.ly/CWins_29

John Michael Morgan, *Brand Against the Machine: How to Build Your Brand, Cut Through the Marketing Noise, and Stand Out from the Competition*, Wiley; 1 edition (November 22, 2011), p. 80.

"I quit my job, wrote 4 books, and started making 6 figures – all without a plan" by Jeff Goins, from Business Insider, April 1, 2015. See http://bit.ly/CWins_30

Chris Ducker, *Rise of the Youpreneur: The Definitive Guide to Becoming the Go-To Leader in Your Industry and Building a Future-Proof Business*, 4C Press (January 30, 2018), p. 11. See also youpreneur.com.

Chapter 7: Identifying your Bullseye Customer

John Michael Morgan, *Brand Against the Machine: How to Build Your Brand, Cut Through the Marketing Noise, and Stand Out from the Competition*, Wiley; 1 edition (November 22, 2011), p. 19.

Peter Drucker in: Philip Kotler *Standing Room Only: Strategies for Marketing the Performing Arts*, Harvard Business Press; (1 January 1997), p. 33.

Philip Kotler, philkotler.com. See http://bit.ly/CWins_31

Chris Guillebeau, chrisguillebeau.com.

Chapter 8: Finding your Superpower

Seth Godin, *Purple Cow*, Portfolio; (2009 edition)

Robert S. Kaplan, *What You're Really Meant to Do: A Road Map for Reaching Your Unique Potential*, Harvard Business Review Press; (May 7, 2013), p. 102.

Chapter 9: Defining your Niche

Michael Port, michaelport.com.

Lee Company, leecompany.com.

Chris Anderson, *The Long Tail: Why the Future of Business Is Selling Less of More*, Hyperion; (2006 edition), p. 40.

Chapter 10: Designing your Offerings

Douglas Karr, dknewmedia.com.

Part 3 Introduction: Activating your referral agents

According to Forrester Research: "How word of mouth is taking marketing to the next level" by Harvey Morris, from WOMMA.org, June 25, 2012. See http://bit.ly/CWins_32

According to Nielsen: "Under the influence" from nielsen.com, September 17, 2013. See http://bit.ly/CWins_33

A Harris poll found that the vast majority: Numbers don't lie: What a 2016 Nielsen study revealed about referrals, by Amity Kapadia, business2community.com, March 12, 2016. See http://bit.ly/CWins_33a

Here's how McKinsey summarized it: "A new way to measure word-of-mouth marketing" by Jacques Bughin, Jonathan Doogan, and Ole Jørgen Vetvik, from McKinsey Quarterly, April 2011. See http://bit.ly/CWins_34

Chapter 11: Be Referral-Worthy

Walt Disney quote. See http://bit.ly/CWins_35

Seth Godin quote. See http://bit.ly/CWins_36

Bob Burg and John David Mann, *The Go-Giver: A surprising way of getting more than you expect*, Portfolio expanded edition (2015), p. 63. See also http://bit.ly/CWins_37

Jay Baer and Daniel Lemin, *Talk Triggers: The Complete Guide to Creating Customers with Word of Mouth*, Portfolio (October 2, 2018), p. 9.

Marcus Sheridan, *They Ask You Answer: A Revolutionary Approach to Inbound Sales, Content Marketing, and Today's Digital Consumer*, Wiley; 1 edition (January 17, 2017), p. 24.

John Jantsch, *The Referral Engine: Teaching your Business to Market Itself*, Portfolio (2010 edition), p. 13.

Chapter 12: Be a Questioner

Tim Sanders, *The Likeability Factor: How to Boost Your L-Factor and Achieve Your Life's Dreams*, Crown Business; Reprint edition (April 25, 2006), p. 180.

Dave Delaney, *New Business Networking: How to Effectively Grow Your Business Network Using Online and Offline Methods* (Que Biz-Tech), Que Publishing; 1 edition (May 26, 2013), p. 21.

Bob Burg, *Endless Referrals*, Third Edition, McGraw-Hill Education; 3 edition (November 15, 2005), p. 21.

Chris Brogan and Julien Smith, *Trust Agents: Using the Web to Build Influence, Improve Reputation, and Earn Trust*, Wiley; 2 edition (August 23, 2010), p. 184.

Chapter 13: Be a Connection Agent

Alana Muller, coffeelunchcoffee.com.

Chris Brogan, chrisbrogan.com.

Keith Ferrazzi, *Never Eat Alone*, Crown Business; second edition (2014), p. 21.

Dorie Clark, *Stand Out: How to Find Your Breakthrough Idea and Build a Following Around It*, Portfolio (April 21, 2015), p. 150-151.

coordinated her rescue: “Leigh Fazzina Bike Crash” from NBC-TV Connecticut on YouTube. See http://bit.ly/CWins_38; see also http://bit.ly/CWins_39 (Twitter recap).

Lisa Petrilli, from Lisa Petrilli Visionary Leadership blog. See http://bit.ly/CWins_40

Chris Brogan and Julien Smith, *Trust Agents: Using the Web to Build Influence, Improve Reputation, and Earn Trust*, Wiley; 2 edition (August 23, 2010), p. 145-146.

Chapter 14: Be Visible

Catherine Morgan, pointatopointbtransitions.com.

Mark Schaefer, businessesgrow.com.

Anthony Iannarino, thesalesblog.com.

Dorie Clark, *Stand Out: How to Find Your Breakthrough Idea and Build a Following Around It*, Portfolio (April 21, 2015), p. 33.

especially in the business realm: "Data-backed insights on whether email marketing is still relevant," from Smart Data Collective, January 20, 2017. See http://bit.ly/CWins_41

Guy Kawasaki, *Enchantment: The Art of Changing Hearts, Minds, and Actions*, Portfolio; Reprint edition (December 31, 2012), p. 2.

Seth Godin, *Tribes: We Need You to Lead Us*, Portfolio; 1 edition (October 16, 2008), p. 15-16.

Chapter 15: Cultivate Advocates

Shiv Singh, quoted in *The Big Book of Business Quotations*, assembled by Johnnie L. Roberts, November 15, 2016.

Jay Baer, *Youtility: Why Smart Marketing Is About Help Not Hype*, Portfolio; Edition (June 27, 2013), p. 30

Tom Martin: conversedigital.com.

Chapter 16: Dominating Niches

Susan Friedman, *Riches in Niches: How to Make it BIG in a Small Market*, Career Press; 1 edition (May 10, 2007).

Aaron Walker, *View From the Top: Living a Life of Significance*, Morgan James Publishing (June 20, 2017), p. 120.

Duct Tape Marketing, ducttapemarketing.com.

Marcus Sheridan, thesaleslion.com.

Five Daughters Bakery, fivedaughtersbakery.com/items.

Benton's Bacon, shop.bentonscountryham.com/aboutus.asp.

Minecraft player Daniel Middleton had over 11 billion views: "The highest-paid YouTube stars 2017," by Madeline Berg, from Forbes, December 7, 2017. See http://bit.ly/CWins_42

Ryan ToysReview now has 10 million subscribers: Ryan Toys Review channel on YouTube. See http://bit.ly/CWins_43

"Joel Comm...made a fortune with farts": from Mixergy.com, July 13, 2018. See http://bit.ly/CWins_44

Jeremy Cowart, jeremycowart.com.

Life Sciences Trainers & Educators Network, l-ten.org.

Chapter 17: Visualizing Opportunities

W. Chan Kim and Renee Mauborgne, *Blue Ocean Strategy: How to Create Uncontested Market Space and Make Competition Irrelevant*, Harvard Business Review Press; 1 edition (February 3, 2005), p. 4.

Don't Panic Management, dontpanicmgmt.com.

Jon Acuff, *Quitter: Closing the Gap Between Your Day Job & Your Dream Job*, Ramsey Press; 4.10.2011 edition (March 3, 2015), p. 228.

Kevin Kruse, kevinkruse.com. See also leadx.org.

Carol Roth, *The Entrepreneur Equation: Evaluating the Realities, Risks, and Rewards of Having Your Own Business*, BenBella Books; 1 edition (March 6, 2012), p. 39.

Chapter 18: Gaining and Maintaining Focus

Tony Robbins, "Where focus goes, energy flows" from tonyrobbins.com. See http://bit.ly/CWins_45

Pamela Wilson, bigbrandsystem.com.

Brian Moran, smallbusinessedge.com.

Steve Jobs (mantra quote), Business Week interview, May 25, 1988. See http://bit.ly/CWins_46

ABOUT THE AUTHOR

Steve Woodruff has often been called the King of Clarity. It's as close to royalty as he's ever gotten.

He's passionate about helping people and businesses see themselves, and articulate themselves, accurately and clearly. Some would say obsessed. They'd be right.

Steve consults with major pharmaceutical companies on their training and communications initiatives, but his greatest joy is helping smaller companies succeed. Thirty-plus years in sales, marketing, leadership, and consulting roles, twelve of those as a solopreneur, have yielded many practical lessons about business success (and failure).

He was a contributing author to the Amazon best-selling book Unstuck, focused on breaking through the barriers to small business growth.

Little-known fact: Steve, at one time, aspired to be an astronomer. Then he ran into college calculus and physics. That experience provided needed clarity about a change in professional direction.

Steve grew up in Connecticut and did his undergraduate work at Vanderbilt University; he and his wife Sandy now reside in Franklin, TN. They have five sons.

Made in the USA
Lexington, KY
22 December 2018